The No-Nonsense Guide to Legal Issues in Web 2.0 and Cloud Computing

The No-Nonsense Guide to Legal Issues in Web 2.0 and Cloud Computing

Charles Oppenheim

f facet publishing

Text © Charles Oppenheim 2012
Index © Bill Johncocks 2012

Published by Facet Publishing
7 Ridgmount Street, London WC1E 7AE
www.facetpublishing.co.uk

Facet Publishing is wholly owned by CILIP: the Chartered
Institute of Library and Information Professionals.

British Library Cataloguing in Publication Data
A catalogue record for this book is available from the British
Library.

ISBN 978-1-85604-804-0

First published 2012

Text printed on FSC accredited material.

Mixed Sources
Product group from well-managed
forests and other controlled sources
www.fsc.org Cert no. SA-COC-1565
© 1996 Forest Stewardship Council
FSC

Typeset from author's files in 10/13 pt Revival 565 and Frutiger
by Flagholme Publishing Services.
Printed and made in Great Britain by MPG Books Group, UK.

Contents

Preface

The internet in general, and Web 2.0 in particular, have become one of the most important means whereby individuals and organizations communicate with one another these days. That communication may be for the purposes of business or pleasure, and may be between people or organizations that know each other, or which have never met before. The result of this dramatic shift in the way people and organizations communicate is the rise of numerous legal problems associated with the use of these new media.

The fundamental problem regarding the legal environment for electronic information creation and communication remains as it always has been: the law is complex, often counter-intuitive, varies from country to country, and almost invariably is behind the times in its technology and the culture of users. Those who interact with such services in their professional capacity, say as librarians, information managers, owners of Web 2.0 services or publishers, therefore have a problem in second-guessing what the law might have to say about particular actions (or lack of action) they might take in regard to the uses they make of the services.

I am not a lawyer. I am a retired academic who has a great interest in the way the law interacts with electronic information. I first got interested in the overlap between the law and information in 1970, when I got involved in patent law and patent information. My interest spread to copyright in 1982, when I got sucked into a fascinating copyright infringement case by accident (ask me about it some time). I got involved in liability for information provision, data protection and electronic information licensing in 1984 through my particular job with what was then called Pergamon Infoline. Again, my job role at the time with Reuters led me into defamation law around 1990. Nowadays, pretty much everything to do with electronic information law is grist to my mill. Nonetheless, I must stress that this book is not a legal textbook aimed at lawyers, but rather, as its title implies, a guide for the perplexed non-lawyer. It should provide a pointer to current issues. It has a focus on Web 2.0, but covers topics relevant to all methods of using electronic information. Nothing in this book is legal advice, and hence the usual caveat. Neither I, nor Facet Publishing, can accept any responsibility for what you do (and choose not to do) as a result of reading this book. If you have any queries relating to the law of information, you need to consult a lawyer. Many large law firms specialize in information law and/or IT law. Some even do not charge excessive fees!

The emphasis of this book is, inevitably, UK and European law, not least because I am not familiar with the laws of other countries, including the USA. But I have tried to draw attention to aspects of US law where possible.

I owe many people my thanks. These include those individuals who took the risk of recruiting me and thereby inadvertently making me aware of information law at various times in the past, including Dennis Caldwell (then of Glaxo), Patrick Gibbins (then of Pergamon Infoline) and Tony Sharp (then of Reuters). Second, I would like to thank Sarah Busby, then of Facet Publishing. Her charm and enthusiasm motivated me to write this book. If she hadn't approached me, this book would never have been written. Next, I would like to thank all those individuals (including many students at the time I was an academic) who have corresponded with me with their legal queries, comments and advice. They are far too many to list, so my apologies for not naming them individually. Next, I would like to acknowledge those authors who have written books I have relied on over the years – many of whom can be found listed in the chapter on further resources. Next, I would like to thank Bill Johncocks, whom I have known for nearly 50 years, for preparing the index to this book. Last, but not least, I would like to thank Adrienne for putting up with me spending hours hitting my keyboard too heavily, and swearing at my computer when drafting chapters.

This book is dedicated to Adrienne, Alfie, Isaac, Joshua, Judith, Lucia and Wendy.

Charles Oppenheim

CHAPTER 1

Introduction

What is Web 2.0?

There are many varied definitions and descriptions of Web 2.0, but the text provided by Wikipedia and adapted below provides an overview.

Web 2.0 provides the user with more user-interface, software and storage facilities. Users can provide the data that is on a Web 2.0 site and exercise some control over that data. These sites may have an 'architecture of participation', which encourages users to add value to the application as they use it.

Web 2.0 offers all users the same freedom to contribute, for good or bad. Characteristics of Web 2.0 are: rich user experience, user participation, dynamic content, metadata, web standards and scalability. Further characteristics, such as openness, freedom and collective intelligence, also known as 'the wisdom of the crowds' by way of user participation, can also be viewed as essential attributes of Web 2.0.

Web 2.0 websites include the following features and techniques:

- *search* – finding information through keyword search
- *links* – connect information together into a meaningful information ecosystem using the model of the web, and provide low-barrier social tools
- *authoring* – the ability to create and update content leads to the collaborative work of many rather than just a few web authors; in wikis, users may extend, undo and redo each other's work; in blogs, posts and the comments of individuals build up over time
- *tags* – categorization of content by users adding 'tags' – short, usually one-word descriptions – to facilitate searching, without dependence on pre-made categories; collections of tags created by many users within a single system are called folksonomies
- *extensions* – software that make the web an application platform as well as a document server; extensions include software like Adobe Reader, Adobe Flash player, Microsoft Silverlight, ActiveX, Oracle Java, Quicktime, Windows Media, and so on

- *signals* – the use of syndication technology such as RSS to notify users of content changes.

A third important part of Web 2.0 is the social web, which is a fundamental shift in the way people communicate. The social web consists of a number of online tools and platforms where people share their perspectives, opinions, thoughts and experiences. Web 2.0 applications tend to interact much more with the user, so the user is not only a user of the application but also a participant by:

- podcasting
- blogging
- tagging
- contributing to RSS
- social bookmarking
- social networking.

The popularity of the term Web 2.0, along with the increasing use of blogs, wikis and social networking technologies, has led many in academia and business to coin a flurry of 2.0s, including Library 2.0, Classroom 2.0, Publishing 2.0 and Government 2.0. Many of these 2.0s refer to Web 2.0 technologies as the source of the new version in their respective disciplines and areas. For example, in the 2006 Talis white paper 'Library 2.0: the challenge of disruptive innovation', Paul Miller argues: 'Blogs, wikis and RSS are often held up as exemplary manifestations of Web 2.0. A reader of a blog or a wiki is provided with tools to add a comment or even, in the case of the wiki, to edit the content. This is what we call the Read/Write web.' (www.capita-libraries.co.uk/resources/documents/447_Library_2_prf1.pdf). Talis believes that Library 2.0 means harnessing this type of participation so that libraries can benefit from increasingly rich collaborative cataloguing efforts, such as including contributions from partner libraries as well as adding rich enhancements, such as book jackets or movie files, to records from publishers and others.

Here, Miller links Web 2.0 technologies and the culture of participation that they engender to the field of library and information management, supporting his claim that there is now a 'Library 2.0'. Many of the other proponents of new 2.0s mentioned here use similar methods.

Web 2.0 offers an opportunity to engage consumers. A growing number of marketers are using Web 2.0 tools to collaborate with consumers on product development, service enhancement and promotion. Companies can use Web 2.0 tools to improve collaboration with their business partners and consumers. Among other things, company employees have created wikis – websites that allow users to add, delete and edit content – to list answers to frequently asked questions about each product, and consumers have added significant contributions. Another marketing Web 2.0 lure is to make sure consumers can use the online community to network among themselves on topics of their own choosing.

Small businesses use Web 2.0 marketing strategies to compete with larger companies. Web 2.0 technologies are used to decrease the gap between businesses and customers. Social networks have become more intuitive and user-friendly. For example, some companies use Twitter to offer customers coupons and discounts for products and services.

Critics of the term claim that 'Web 2.0' does not represent a new version of the web at all, but merely continues to use established web technologies and concepts. They say the technology is not novel, and that many of the ideas of Web 2.0 had already been featured in implementations on networked systems well before the term emerged. Amazon, for instance, has allowed users to write reviews since 1995. Amazon also opened its application programming interface to outside developers in 2002. The most common criticism is that the term is unclear or simply a buzzword. For example, in a podcast interview in 2006, Tim Berners-Lee described the term 'Web 2.0' as a 'piece of jargon': 'Nobody really knows what it means. . . . If Web 2.0 for you is blogs and wikis, then that is people to people. But that was what the Web was supposed to be all along.' (www.ibm.com/developerworks/podcast/dwi/cm-int082206txt.html).

Web 2.0 allows anybody, anywhere, to share and, by implication, place undue value on their own opinions about any subject and post any kind of content, regardless of their knowledge, credentials, biases or hidden agendas. The core assumption of Web 2.0, that all opinions and user-generated content are equally valuable and relevant, is arguably misguided. *Sunday Times* reviewer John Flintoff has (2007) characterized Web 2.0 as 'creating an endless digital forest of mediocrity: uninformed political commentary, unseemly home videos, embarrassingly amateurish music, unreadable poems, essays and novels', and also asserted that Wikipedia is full of 'mistakes, half truths and misunderstandings' (http://technology.timesonline.co.uk/tol/news/tech_and_web/personal_tech/arti cle1874668.ece). Michael Gorman, former president of the American Library Association and a well known critic of some modern computerized retrieval systems, has been particularly vocal in his opposition to Web 2.0. He argues (2007) that the lack of expertise of those who contribute damages the usefulness of, for example, social networking sites. However, he believes that there is some hope for the future: 'The task before us is to extend into the digital world the virtues of authenticity, expertise, and scholarly apparatus that have evolved over the 500 years of print, virtues often absent in the manuscript age that preceded print.' (www.britannica.com/blogs/2007/06/web-20-the-sleep-of-reason-part-i/).

But despite the apparent decline in the use of the term in recent years, 'Web

2.0' has become a convenient and widely applied term for all applications on the web that involve user participation, as opposed to simply users sucking information out.

Legal issues of Web 2.0

Library and information professionals already have many sources of information about Web 2.0 applications through books (there are dozens listed on the Amazon bookstore), professional and scholarly publications, and conferences. The legal issues associated with library and information work are well known and well served by books. So why yet another book on Web 2.0, but this time focusing on legal issues? Surely Web 2.0 applications do not alter the legal landscape? Well, not quite. There are numerous reasons why library and information professionals need to be aware of the novel legal issues associated with Web 2.0:

1. Web 2.0 is international. Unlike traditional library and information management operations, which tend to be conducted within a single country, and are therefore subject to the laws of that one country, with Web 2.0, contributors of materials potentially come from all over the world, and the materials resulting from the Web 2.0 application tend to get distributed all over the world. This book is primarily focused on UK law, and to a lesser extent, European Union (EU) and US law. Although many of the broad principles apply in other countries as well, there will always be a nagging worry that something on a Web 2.0 service that is perfectly legal in one country will break another country's laws. Unfortunately, this book cannot give authoritative advice on the information-related laws of countries around the world, but it can remind you of the issues that are likely to arise.

2. Anyone can contribute – unlike most library and information technical applications, in Web 2.0 the range of people able to contribute is much wider than just a group of professionals with all the high standards one associates with that term. Many of those contributing to a Web 2.0 service are either ignorant of, or contemptuous of, established laws, and so the chances of something illegal being disseminated on a Web 2.0 service are that much higher.

3. The lines of responsibility are blurred – whereas in the past, it was clear who was responsible for creating and disseminating particular data or information, that distinction is less clear when the people contributing may be using pseudonyms or become totally anonymous, and where it is unclear who or what helped the illegal material (if it is illegal) be spread to all the readers. Furthermore, in many cases, what is posted is the product of

collaboration between several contributors, and it might be difficult or impossible to tease out who was responsible for what bit.

4. New legal issues arise in Web 2.0 that one does not associate with traditional library technologies. To give one example, those who contribute to Twitter or to Facebook may well be putting their own jobs or careers at risk by posting material that brings their employer or themselves into disrepute. There are issues to do with contract formation, stalking and harassment, gambling, advertising, VAT, liability and other legal problems, which can arise in Web 2.0 and which the library and information manager may never have encountered before.

5. Although the technology of Web 2.0 is well established, the law has yet to catch up – contract law, liability law, defamation law, internet scams law and copyright law are all struggling to keep up with the activities and norms of Web 2.0 users. This leads to uncertainty and/or a black hole because the law cannot cope (see for example the laws on spamming) and/or laws are over-zealous (see for example the attempts by legislators to cut copyright infringement with more and more draconian laws – which are either ignored, or bypassed with technical fixes by those determined to keep on infringing, or who object in principle to any kind of censorship).

6. There are also numerous extra problems thrown up by cloud computing. Many Web 2.0 applications run on cloud computing facilities; of course, there are many 'Web 1.0' applications running on cloud computing as well. In this book, two particular issues relevant to cloud computing are highlighted: the diffuse geographical basis of cloud computing, and the one-sided nature of the contracts imposed by cloud computing services; both cause potential problems. These are explored more fully in Chapter 7.

The structure of this book

This book comprises eight chapters (including this one). They cover copyright, other intellectual property rights (IPRs), data protection and privacy, freedom of information, defamation, liability issues and cloud computing. There is a brief annotated bibliography of works and websites that I have found useful. The list in the bibliography is not intended to be comprehensive.

Readers will find case studies and exercises scattered in many of the chapters. Generally, the case studies relate to real events, though sometimes they are hypothetical. The questions in the exercises are designed to help you think through the issues raised. Suggested answers can be found towards the end of each chapter, but it is worth stressing that many legal scenarios are open to different interpretations and conclusions. If you disagree with the answers provided, e-mail me at c.oppenheim@btinternet.com!

The text represents my understanding of the law at the middle of 2012. Obviously the law constantly changes, as does the interpretation of the law by courts. Readers should bear this in mind when considering the implications of the advice provided in this book. This leads on to the disclaimer already mentioned in the Preface that all readers should bear in mind: I am not a lawyer, and I can accept no responsibility for any actions you choose to take (or not take) as a result of reading this book. If you are in any doubt at all about a legal matter, my advice is simple – talk to a lawyer!

CHAPTER 2

Copyright

Introduction

The focus of library and information professionals is the handling of information, increasingly these days in electronic form. They are concerned with the creation, dissemination, storage, retrieval, curation and disposal of said information. All these activities involve copyright issues, and it is for this reason that copyright looms so large in the concerns of the professionals. There is therefore no apology for the fact that this chapter, on copyright issues in Web 2.0, is the longest in this book. The chapter examines how one acquires copyright, the vexed question of copyright ownership, the types of materials protected by copyright, the lifetime of copyright works, the restricted acts that only the rights holder can authorize (or refuse to authorize), and issues to do with infringement and how to copy third party materials legally. There is also a discussion on orphan works, differences between UK law and other laws, and recent developments in UK copyright law. Sections of the chapter focus on where copyright law interacts with Web 2.0.

Recent developments, such as the UK's 2010 Digital Economy Act (discussed further below), have highlighted the tensions between copyright owners and users of copyright works in the current environment of ready availability of machine readable material and contempt for old-fashioned business models among the young. Information professionals are caught up in this tension. They are all keen to respect copyright, but at the same time are finding that governments are passing legislation that hinders rather than helps them in their professional roles.

UK copyright law is governed by the 1988 Copyright, Designs and Patents Act (hereinafter called the CDPA). Despite its title, the Act says relatively little about the law of patents or registered designs, but it is the key piece of legislation on copyright. Nonetheless, the CDPA is not the only piece of legislation of relevance. Numerous statutory instruments, such as the snappily titled Copyright (Librarians and Archivists) (Copying of Copyright Materials) Regulations 1989, supplement the CDPA, and some other primary legislation, such as the Public Lending Right Act 1979 and the Digital Economy Act 2010 are also relevant.

The CDPA is an incredibly complex piece of legislation, having grown organically (thanks mainly to the incorporation of EU directives of relevance into it) over the years since it was first passed. Its sections are numbered 1 to 306, but there are numerous sections with numbers plus letters, such as Section 296ZF, so that in total there are about 400 sections, not to mention five schedules. The CDPA is probably the best cure for insomnia yet invented, and indeed the complexity of the Act, the fact that it is now out of date, taking too little account as it does of developments in technology (in particular the internet) and cultural attitudes, together with much ambiguous wording in the Act itself, are good reasons why so many people avoid studying it, but are worried by the law and its implications for their working and personal lives.

The legislation at a glance

The CDPA is the major piece of legislation covering UK copyright law. As noted above, it has been amended many times since 1988. It is therefore important that if you are consulting it, you use the latest version of the Act.

Statutory instruments associated with the CDPA are also important in some areas. Thus, for example, SI 1989/1212 is a key piece of legislation for librarians and archivists making copies for patrons, while SI 1995/3297 is important on the lifetime of copyright.

The original text of some EU directives (for example, the directive on database right, and the so-called Information Society Directive) is also sometimes important. Although the directives have been incorporated into UK law, the preambles in those directives often give important clues regarding the intention of the EU, and such preambles do get revisited in court cases from time to time. Furthermore, key cases are often decided at the European Court of Justice, whose decisions often are imposed on the UK courts.

The Public Lending Right Act 1979 and associated statutory instruments are important in this area of library operations.

The Digital Economy Act 2010, if implemented in the form it was originally worded when passed, could have major implications for those running Web 2.0 services. If users of the service are regularly uploading or downloading infringing materials, the organization running the service could find itself in the firing line and possibly having to close its services down following complaints by aggrieved copyright owners.

The ambiguity of the wording in the CDPA (for example, the words 'substantial' and 'substantially' appear numerous times in the Act without being defined) is deliberate, it is claimed by some, to encourage the development of licences between rights owners and users of copyright works. Similarly, some of the definitions in the Digital Economy Act 2010 (of 'internet service provider – ISP' and 'subscriber' in particular) are so poorly drafted that it is difficult for many organizations to decide if they are an ISP, a subscriber, both or neither. I'm more inclined towards the cock-up theory of such poorly drafted legislation; copyright is by its very nature an attempt to address the tension between those who own rights, and wish to make money from exploiting those rights, and those that wish to use copyright materials with a minimum of formality and (ideally) for nothing. In trying to address this tension, and at the same time not really understanding the changes in technology and cultural attitudes, the parliamentary draughtsmen have produced monsters that are sometimes out of date, take no account of cultural attitudes, and are ambiguous and often incomprehensible.

Despite its name, copyright is not, in fact, the right to copy something. Rather, it is the right of the copyright owner to either authorize, or refuse to authorize, the copying (or the doing of certain other things, discussed later – see the section 'Restricted acts') of a copyright work. In addition, the copyright owner (or, under some circumstances, someone authorized by them) has the right to sue for copyright infringement if someone has undertaken restricted acts on their copyright work without their permission. Infringement is discussed further below, as are exceptions to copyright, which allow the performance of restricted acts legally under certain restricted circumstances.

In order to enjoy copyright (lawyers use the term 'in order for copyright to subsist', but since 'subsist' is not a word in common use, it is not used here), the work must be *new*. Different countries use different standards to decide whether a particular work is new or not. In some countries, especially in continental Europe, 'new' implies some degree of intellectual creativity, whereas in the UK, in general the basis of being 'new' is simply 'not copied from something else'.

It is often said that copyright protects not the idea behind a work, but only the expression of that work in a fixed form. Thus it is the effort in executing the work that is required to get copyright. The presence or absence of originality or creativity of thought behind that act of execution is irrelevant.

Case study A

A person takes a snapshot of a building. No particular skill or technique is involved. Under UK law, the photograph enjoys copyright because it is new – it is not copied. However, under some continental European laws, because there was no particular skill involved in setting up the camera and checking the lighting, the photograph might not enjoy copyright. Similarly, if someone scans in some text in a digitization project, it is not certain that the product of the scanning process enjoys copyright in UK law or not. Arguably, it is simply a copy, and therefore does not enjoy copyright. But if skill were applied to the setting up of the scanner and the placing of the document to ensure maximum resolution of the scan, there definitely would be copyright.

In continental Europe, there would have to be evidence of considerable skill and expertise being used before such a scan would enjoy copyright.

In addition to having to be something new, the work, in order to enjoy copyright, must be *fixed in some tangible form*. Thus, if someone makes an extempore speech, and no one is recording that speech in any way, whether by means of audiovisual equipment or by making a full transcript, that speech does not enjoy copyright. But as soon as it is recorded in some fixed format (which could be in a variety of media, including shorthand or sound recording), it will enjoy copyright. This fixation requirement does not imply permanence. The matter might have been fixed for only a short period of time and still would enjoy copyright. Incidentally, there is no requirement that the person who created the material is also the person who fixed it, and it is immaterial whether the fixation had the creator's consent or not.

Case study B
If I make an extempore speech and someone else without my agreement tape-records it, then there is a copyright work (a sound recording – see below) and the creators were both I as the speaker and the person who made the recording. We then have joint ownership of the copyright in the recording. Joint ownership is discussed further below.

WEB 2.0 POINT
Works that Web 2.0 users encounter are indeed fixed in some way, whether originally in print, as electronic records or as audiovisual media of some kind.

The formalities needed to get copyright
This subheading is misleading. No formalities are required for copyright to be acquired. Copyright is automatically created as soon as the creator creates something new! There is no need to register, pay fees or fill out any forms. Thus, services that claim to offer copyright registration for a fee are not needed. The only circumstance where registration might be useful is in the USA, where, in order to sue for the infringement of copyright, one needs to have registered the copyright with the US authorities.

The fact that there is no need to go through any formalities might make one wonder why so many items have a © followed by the name of the copyright owner and a date – as indeed does this book. The use of this symbol, while not in any way affecting the owner's right to claim copyright or to sue for infringement, is useful because it acts as a warning to would-be infringers. In effect, it says, 'Watch out! I know about copyright and will sue if you infringe.' It is also useful to display such symbols if the work is going to be disseminated in those few countries that are party to the Universal Copyright Convention but not the Berne Convention (see below), as the symbol is necessary if one is to pursue an infringement action in those countries.

To sum up: all that is required to obtain copyright is that the material created is not copied, and that it should be fixed in some way or another. There is just one exception to this basic rule: to gain copyright in a database, there should be some degree of creativity applied in the selection or arrangement of the materials within the database.

Furthermore, statements along the lines 'All rights reserved. No part of this work may be copied, stored in an information retrieval system or reproduced without the permission of the copyright owner' have little standing in law. That is why, as in this book, the publisher has added the key words 'Except as otherwise permitted under the Copyright Designs and Patents Act 1988'. Licences and contracts can over-ride the law of copyright under certain circumstances, as long as the person wishing to use the material being offered has agreed to the licence terms in advance. A person who only sees these licence terms *after* they have bought or borrowed the work is not necessarily bound by those terms and conditions. Rather it is the law that decides in these circumstances what one can or cannot do with the copyright work. As we shall see, there *are* some circumstances when a user can copy a copyright work without having to ask for permission or pay a fee, so that is the legal position if someone purchases or borrows a work without having agreed to particular terms and conditions in advance. The use of the phrase 'All rights reserved' is, however, useful because it confirms that the rights owner is aware that they own a number of rights associated with copyright, that they are holding all of them, and reserve the right to sue for infringement if any of the rights are infringed. This emphasizes an important point: ownership of copyright involves the ownership of a bundle of rights (explained in the section 'Restricted acts') and, what is more, they apply in all the major countries of the world (see below). The owner is perfectly entitled to grant permission based on sub-sets of those rights and in sub-sets of the world, for example, 'I grant you permission to copy this work in Argentina.'

If a copyright work is prefaced with the statement 'All rights reserved. *Except as permitted under the Copyright, Designs and Patents Act 1988,* no one may copy, store in an information retrieval system or disseminate this work', this is perfectly acceptable, as the words in italics are stating that the law is what decides what you can or cannot do with the work.

Because the UK is a signatory to the two major international copyright conventions (known as the Berne Convention and the Universal Copyright Convention), as soon as a copyright work is created in the UK, it automatically gets protection in all other countries that are signatories to these conventions (in practice, that means virtually every country in the world). Equally, if, say, a creator creates something new in (say) Singapore, they automatically get copyright protection for that material in the UK. The Berne Convention requires higher minimum protection standards for copyright owners than the Universal Copyright Convention and, indeed, the UK's level of protection for rights owners is in many regards even stronger than Berne's minimum requirements. In addition, the UK is a member of the World Trade Organization (WTO), and has signed up to its TRIPS (Trade Related Aspects of Intellectual Property Rights) Agreement, which places further obligations on the UK Government regarding lifetime of copyright, various related rights, exceptions to copyright (see below), enforcement measures when dealing with infringement, criminal procedures and procedures for settling disputes between WTO member states. Again, the UK law fulfils its numerous obligations under TRIPS. There are a number of less important international conventions with relevance to copyright, which the UK is signed up to, and in addition there is a proposed new international convention called ACTA (Anti-Counterfeiting Trade Agreement), which is under consideration by the EU. If passed, it would increase the obligations on member states to enforce and prosecute for copyright infringement in the future.

It is also worth stressing that because of these international conventions, one has only to consider the law as it applies to the country in which an action such as alleged infringement took place.

Case study C

An e-book created and sold from the USA is being used in the UK. The user is copying its contents and passing it to friends because of a fault in the e-books digital rights management system, which should have prevented such actions. *Prima facie* there is copyright infringement occurring. It is UK not US law that applies, because the alleged infringement took place in the UK.

Case study D

The law regarding making copies for educational purposes is far more generous in the USA than it is in the UK. Gemma is a teacher who is visiting the USA on holiday, and comes across a textbook that she uses in her teaching. She decides to make 50 copies of a key chapter using a copy shop in the USA. Let us assume this is legal in the USA, but not in the UK. She then flies back to the UK, carrying the 50 sets of photocopies in her luggage. She has, in fact, broken the law, because, as will be shown below, it is an offence to import materials into the UK if it would have been infringement to copy them in the UK. However, the legal position becomes messier when discussing networked materials. What if Michael, based in the UK, sends an instruction to a computer in Singapore, making that computer send to a person in South Africa a scanned copy of a book, and what if such an action would be illegal in the UK and in South Africa, but is legal in Singapore. Whose law applies? Legal experts cannot agree on this matter. It would not be important if all countries' copyright laws were identical, but they are not. They are similar, but not identical, so anomalies like this can arise.

WEB 2.0 POINT
Users of Web 2.0 materials should always work on the assumption that third party materials they include are subject to copyright, and that anything they create and add to the Web 2.0 application is also protected by copyright. Web 2.0 users are generally both creators of copyright materials and users of third party copyright materials.

Ownership of copyright
The *first* owner of the copyright in a work is *normally* the person who created the work. The two words in italics need further explanation. Copyright is one of a group of legal entities known as 'intellectual property rights' (or IPRs). The word 'property' is significant; just as with physical property (such as a house), if one owns an IPR, one can sell it, rent it out, mortgage it, pass it on to ones' heirs when one dies, and so on. Thus, the initial owner of copyright might choose to sell it, or give it away for free (the legal term for either action is *assign* it) to someone else. To be legally valid, an assignment must be in writing.

Case study E
An author writes a work of fiction and decides to make money from it by selling it to a publisher. They might choose to assign copyright in it to the publisher in return for a fixed fee, or for royalties based on a percentage of sales. Either way, having assigned the copyright, the author no longer has any say in the work, as it is the publisher who owns the copyright. Nonetheless, as we shall see, the lifetime of the copyright is linked to the date the author dies, so the publisher has a vested interest in ensuring that the author has a long and healthy life.

The pop singer Lady Gaga requires that anyone photographing her assigns copyright in those photographs to her. This is despite the fact that a photographer initially owns the copyright in photographs they take. Lady Gaga is engaging in not untypical behaviour for major sports and media personalities. There is nothing illegal about her demands, but, as with all copyright assignments, they must be signed to be legally valid.

The point that should be emphasized is that normally the creator owns the copyright in what they create. The reason for the word 'normally' is that there are exceptions to the rule that the first owner is the creator. If someone creates a work as part of his or her employee duties, then (unless there is a contract of employment that says something different) it is the employer who owns the copyright, not the employee. But what exactly is an employee and what are that employee's normal duties?

Case study F

An employee is paid to write press releases for their employer. The copyright in those press releases automatically belongs to the employer. But if the employee chooses to spend their time writing poems, the copyright in those poems, even if written in work time and using the employer's equipment, belongs to the employee, as they were not paid to write poems. The employer is of course entitled to dismiss the employee for not doing their job, but he or she cannot claim ownership of the copyright in the poems.

An employee's normal duties can be found in that employee's contract of employment. Unfortunately, many employees' contracts are rather vaguely worded, for example, stating, 'you shall do such duties as your manager reasonably requires of you'. This can lead to problems when copyright ownership disputes arise.

WEB 2.0 POINT

In November 2011, a court in England issued an order that required an employee who resigned to start his own consulting business to turn over all of his LinkedIn contacts to his former employer, along with proof that none of them became clients of his new firm. This result is not surprising. The list was without doubt created as part of the employee's duties. While copyright in an employee's LinkedIn profile probably belongs to the individual, their contact list does not.

In 2010, in an unrelated case, the Eastern District Court of New York state ruled in *Sasqua Group, Inc. v. Courtney* that the availability of information in social media invalidated the company's argument that the information was a trade secret.

There also may be occasions when it is unclear whether the person is an employee or not. Freelancers and temporary staff are definitely not employees, but the position of part-time staff or peripatetic staff can be problematic. In general, freelancers who are paid to carry out duties for someone, but are not employees, own the copyright in anything they produce, though some court cases have disagreed with this simple approach, suggesting that the freelancer has granted the person commissioning the work at minimum an implied licence to copy the work.

Case study G

A freelance software writer is paid £5000 by an organization to develop a piece of software for them. The software is successfully completed, and the organization pays the money. Because the freelancer is not an employee in the normal sense of the word (for example, there is no contract of employment, rather a contract for services, the organization does not pay a contribution to the freelancer's National Insurance, and there are no paid holidays), unless there is a written assignment of copyright, it is unclear whether the organization that commissioned the work owns the copyright in the software, has a licence to copy and use it but does not own it, or has no rights at all to the software. For these reasons, it is always best that as part of the contract between the freelancer and the organization there is a clause that explicitly assigns copyright in the resulting software to the organization commissioning the work.

Exercise 1

Fred is employed by his college to undertake teaching duties. Fred develops handouts, PowerPoints, tests and exams (with answers) to this end. Fred is then offered, and chooses to accept, a job in another college, teaching the same subject. Who owns the copyright in the materials Fred has created? Can Fred take all these teaching materials with him to the new employer? Is Fred's previous employer entitled to insist that copies remain with that college?

WEB 2.0 POINT

Consider a Web 2.0 product developed by a member of staff. Was it created as part of employee duties? If so, the copyright in the contribution may well be owned by the employer. If, on the other hand, it is clearly extraneous to employee duties (or indeed, if the person in question is a freelancer), then probably the copyright in the materials will be owned by the contributor. In the case of a typical Web 2.0 application with multiple contributors, perhaps from many countries, the copyright ownership of whatever results is complex. There may well be multiple owners. It might therefore be helpful to get all contributors to agree to either assign copyright, or grant a free of charge licence, to whatever organization is 'hosting' or leading the Web 2.0 application. Getting all contributors to agree to this may be easier said than done though.

It should also be noted that students are not employees of their educational establishment, so own the copyright in any coursework, exam answers and so on that they prepare. Legal opinion states that any attempt by an educational establishment to insist that it is a condition of taking a student on the programme that the student assigns copyright to the educational institution would be regarded by the courts as an unfair contractual term. The best the educational institution can do is to *invite* the student to assign or license materials they produce for use by the institution, and not to penalize any student who declines that invitation.

However, there is no requirement for an educational establishment to return students' work to them. This emphasizes a key point: *physical ownership of a copyright work is not the same as copyright ownership of that work.* Just because someone owns a book, a painting, a record and so on does not entitle them to act as a copyright owner and does not entitle them, for example, to make further copies.

Case study H

A tabloid newspaper receives a bundle of letters sent by the late Princess Diana to a confidante in the 1980s, and plans to reproduce them. Following a legal complaint by Prince Harry and Prince William, the newspaper is prevented from doing so, as it is not the copyright owner. The copyright is no longer owned by Princess Diana, as she is dead, but by the heirs and successors of Princess Diana, and only they can authorize the making of copies. Equally, though, the newspaper is not under any obligation to pass the letters to the princes. It is entitled to retain physical ownership.

There are many cases where joint ownership of a copyright work occurs. This is normally when it is impossible to ascertain which parts of the work one person created and which by another. This is not unusual in the copyright world, but causes problems for those who wish to reproduce the work, as they have to get the agreement of all the owners before they can proceed.

WEB 2.0 POINT

Many Web 2.0 products incorporate jointly owned copyright materials. This is particularly true in the case of wikis, but could also apply where there has been collaboration in social bookmarking, social documents or virtual worlds. This inevitably causes problems if permissions are requested to reproduce these products, as it may not be possible to identify all the joint authors to get their permission. In order for permission to be granted, all the joint owners need to give their agreement.

Even where it is clear that a Web 2.0 product consists of separate individually owned items (for example, a collection of microblogging posts), there will still be some problems in approaching each contributor in turn for permission to copy if someone wishes to reproduce the entire discussion thread.

Types of copyright materials

The major types of works that are protected by copyright are: literary works, dramatic works, musical works, artistic works, sound recordings, films, radio and TV broadcasts and typography and layout.

Literary works comprise anything that is recorded in writing, including printed works, handwritten works, plus anything in machine-readable form (because they are stored as a series of 1s and 0s in a computer memory, and numbers are indeed a form of writing). There is no implication of literary merit; thus even a dreadfully written student essay is still a literary work in law. Literary works also include tables and compilations (and separately, databases – see Chapter 3; the distinction need not detain us here), computer programs and preparatory designs for a computer program. The legal definition requires that the literary work must be written, spoken or sung. However, short sentences, single words, names or titles rarely enjoy copyright because they are too short to be considered a literary work. Quite when a string of characters is long enough to become a literary work would be considered on a case-by-case basis.

Case study I

A recent European Court of Justice ruling stated that a string of 11 words was capable of being a literary work.

WEB 2.0 POINT

Anything stored in a computer is a literary work, and so anything stored in a Web 2.0 application will be a literary work while stored. It may well be a film, sound recording and so on, as well. One of the problems with digitized materials is that they may fall under the headings of several media types simultaneously. This makes clearing rights – getting permission to copy – complex.

Dramatic works are separate from literary works, and relate to works that are capable of being performed to the public. In other words, there are actions associated with the performance, and the instructions (for example, 'exit stage left') form part of the dramatic work. Thus, a dramatic work comprises dialogue and acting directions. If the dramatic work includes music, the music is subject to separate copyright, as described below. By definition in the CDPA, a dramatic work is never a literary work, and a literary work is never a dramatic work.

Musical works are, in essence, musical scores using some kind of notation. As with literary works, there is no implication of musical merit.

Case study J

A passage of silence, such as John Cage's famous piece *4' 33"*, is incidentally not a musical work (because it is silence) and is therefore not protected by copyright. Stories you may have heard about John Cage threatening to sue for infringement of his silent composition are now known to have been hoaxes.

A piece of music comprising notes and lyrics is a combination of a musical work (notation) and literary work (lyrics).

> **WEB 2.0 POINT**
> The only time a musical work is likely to be encountered in Web 2.0 is where sheet music has been scanned in. A recording of music played in a Web 2.0 application is indeed still copyright (assuming copyright has not expired in it), but as a sound recording. Performers' rights (see below) may well also be involved.

Artistic works again have no implication of artistic merit. They include anything to be looked at, such as drawings, paintings, diagrams, photographs, paintings, maps, charts, engravings, woodcuts, typefaces, sculptures, collages, works of architecture (including models of buildings and the buildings themselves), pottery and embroidery.

> **WEB 2.0 POINT**
> Artistic works are very likely to be present in a Web 2.0 application. A good example of a Web 2.0 application with many artistic works is Flickr.

Sound recordings are protected, whether in analogue or digital form. The definition of this media type is extremely broad, and it covers, in essence, anything that can be heard when played back.

> **WEB 2.0 POINT**
> Sound recordings are quite likely to be present in a Web 2.0 application. Some major sound archives, such as the National Sound Archive run by the British Library, contain many sound recordings.

Films are defined as any medium from which a moving image can be reproduced, including analogue and digital formats. Thus, both video recordings and DVDs containing moving images are considered to be films.

> **WEB 2.0 POINT**
> Films are very likely to be present in a Web 2.0 application, whether they are films in the popular sense of the term, or any other moving images. Films heavily populate YouTube, which is a classic Web 2.0 service.

Broadcasts can be made on radio or TV, and can be transmitted by wireless means or by cable. They cover any electronic transmission of visual images and/or sounds and/or data intended for wide simultaneous distribution to members of the public.

WEB 2.0 POINT
Broadcasts may well be present in a Web 2.0 application. In some services, such as YouTube, they are very common.

Finally, there is special protection for *typographical arrangements of published editions*. This protects the layout and presentation of such printed or hand-written works.

WEB 2.0 POINT
Typographical editions will in general only be present in a Web 2.0 application when some printed text has been scanned in.

It will be clear from this discussion that, other than when specifically taken into account (for example, a dramatic work cannot in UK law be a literary work, and vice versa), any given creation could fall under more than one of these headings. Thus, for example, a fiction book with illustrations has protection as a literary work and an artistic work, and the typographical layout is protected. A more complex example can be found in the case of a DVD of *The Sound of Music*. This is a film, but also a dramatic work, it also has musical copyright and literary copyright in the songs and lyrics, and the DVD cover will have literary and artistic copyright, plus protection for the typographical layout of the cover text. There are also performers' rights, discussed in Chapter 3, involved. There may well be computer programs involved for running the DVD, and if the DVD comes with extras (as many DVDs do), there may be database rights involved as well as separate copyright in the extra materials.

Now such complexity would not be a problem if the ground rules for each media type were the same, but they are not. The rules about the ownership and lifetime of copyright, what can and cannot be done with the work without having to ask for permission, and the culture of the different industries when permission is sought for reproduction, are so different that multimedia works cause extreme problems to those wishing to make copies or otherwise exploit them. Unfortunately, it is most unlikely that we will ever reach a situation where the ground rules for these matters become uniform.

WEB 2.0 POINT
By definition, Web 2.0 applications involve materials in machine-readable

form, but these could include all the media types listed above. However, while such materials are stored on a computer memory somewhere (whether on hard disc, a flash memory stick or on a cloud application), they will be at minimum a literary work, as they comprise a series of 1s and 0s.

One should work on the basis that everything in machine-readable form is subject to copyright. This of course implies that anything created within a Web 2.0 environment enjoys copyright. Thus, Web 2.0 materials will include copyright materials owned by the contributors, as well as potentially infringing third party owned copyright materials.

Lifetime of copyright

Virtually every work has a limited copyright lifetime in UK law (the exceptions are so rare as not to justify consideration here). After that lifetime, the work is said to fall 'in the public domain' and anything can be done with it, for example, copying it. Nonetheless, the majority of materials encountered in Web 2.0 environments are likely to be in copyright. Confusingly, the lifetime varies from one type of work to another. For example, the duration of copyright in a published literary, dramatic, musical or artistic work is usually 70 years from the end of the year that the creator (or the last of its creators if jointly authored) died. This life plus 70 years is common for a lot of media, but not all media. Among those media types with non-standard durations are unpublished literary works (such as manuscripts or letters), unpublished photographs, works created by HM Government, employee-created works (for example, created by a company), sound recordings, broadcasts, computer-generated works and typographical arrangements. Readers should check standard textbooks, or indeed CDPA Sections 12–15, to check the lifetime of works they are interested in.

The EU recently passed a directive extending the life of copyright in sound recordings from 50 years from the date of the recording to 70 years from the recording date. If the recording is of music, lyrics, a play, poetry and so on, the lifetime of copyright in that work is now (once the directive is converted into UK law) 70 years from the date of the recording, or 70 years after the death of the creator of the lyrics, music, poetry and so on, whichever is the later. If there is no authored music, lyrics and so on, for example, a sound recording of birdsong, then the lifetime is now 70 years from the date of the recording.

In the case of published works (and 'published' here has the common-sense definition of copies being made available to the public, or a sub-set of the public, whether for a fee or not), it is reasonable to assume that anything more than 120 years old is likely to be out of copyright. There will be the odd exception of a work published by someone when the author was very young, and the author went on to live to a very great age, but this would be a low-risk working approach. Note that even when an item is in the public domain, the physical owner of the item is not obliged to let any third party make copies of it. There may be good reasons, for example, to preserve a fragile original, for a library, archive or other owner to refuse to let a third party make copies of the work. It is for this reason, for example, that many art galleries refuse to allow people to take photographs of paintings and other artistic works, whether or not they are out of copyright.

Exercise 2

The author George Orwell died on 21 January 1950. When will the copyright to his published books expire? Do you need to check with whoever he assigned copyright to before being sure? What practical impact will such an expiry have?

Restricted acts – or what can you do or not do to a copyright work?

As noted earlier, the copyright owner has the right to authorize, or to refuse to authorize, the copying (and certain other things) of its copyright work. These so-called restricted acts (in the sense that only the copyright owner can authorize them) comprise the following activities:

- copying the work
- issuing copies of the work to the public (or a sub-set of the public)
- renting or lending the work (though libraries have certain permissions to do so)
- performing, showing or playing the work to the public
- broadcasting the work
- adapting or amending the work in some certain ways
- importing the work knowing it to be infringing
- using electronic means to communicate the work to the public.

Some of these terms need further explanation.

The *reproduction right* is the best-known and most obvious right – the right to authorize or refuse to authorize the copying of the work. This right, like all the other rights, applies not just to the entire work, but to a 'substantial part' of the work as well. 'Substantial' is measured just as much by quality or importance as it is by quantity. Thus, a very small proportion of the original work might be copied, but if what is copied is important to that work, then a substantial amount has been copied. This could be as little as a few lines of code in a complete computer program, a few bars of a song, or a key sentence in a literary work. The copying can be transient or permanent – either requires the permission of the copyright owner.

WEB 2.0 POINT
Most Web 2.0 applications include copies of copyright works, and so may well infringe copyright if the copying has been done without permission.

Exercise 3
Leanne wishes to reproduce one sentence from a detective story in a discussion she is publishing on the detective story genre. The line in question is 'Yes, I admit I murdered Lord Bottomley, sobbed Colonel Mustard.' This is ten words out a 100,000-word book, or 0.01% of the length. Is this substantial?

WEB 2.0 POINT
Many Web 2.0 products are largely user-created but may contain very small portions of third party material. The question then arises whether the copying that has occurred is 'substantial'.

Another problem associated with Web 2.0 is that users who generate content in a Web 2.0 application often are ignorant of, or indifferent or hostile to, the whole concept of copyright. This clearly raises risks for the administrators of the Web 2.0 product, who may not realistically be able to police what is being posted.

The *distribution right* is the right to issue physical copies to the public. This refers only to the initial distribution of the work. There is, for example, nothing to stop a *bona fide* purchaser of a work from further distributing it by, for example, re-selling the work, or giving it to a charity shop. The situation is more complex when the purchaser has licensed the item from the seller, for example, has obtained a licence for an e-book. In such cases, the purchaser must abide by the rules of the licence when considering further distribution – and many licences prohibit such further distribution.

As so often in copyright law, 'public' here means the general public, or any sub-set of the public.

WEB 2.0 POINT
The risk in putting materials onto a Web 2.0 application is probably more to do with communication to the public (see below) than with the distribution right, which is about the distribution of physical copies. For this reason, this particular restricted act is not considered further here.

The *rental and lending right* refers to systematic rental (for money) or lending (not for money) of copies of the work to the public. It does not stop an individual lending a work to a friend. Lending of books by public and other so-called prescribed libraries is not an infringement either. A prescribed library in UK law is, very simplistically, a library associated with an educational establishment, a government department, a learned society, a library associated with the NHS (National Health Service), and a few other not-for-profit libraries. Readers who work in libraries should consult copyright textbooks for further advice on the status of their library. In UK law, it is also legal for any educational establishment to lend copies of works held by it to any third party. Issues to do with rental and lending are unlikely to arise in a Web 2.0 context.

The *performance right* applies to literary, dramatic or musical works, and includes lectures, speeches and the performing of sound recordings, films and broadcasts of the work. Again, the act is in relation to the public or some sub-set of the public. *If the Web 2.0 application includes any kind of recording of a performance, it may well infringe this right.*

Case study K

The owners of the rights to *Charlotte's Web* refused permission for the recitation of two paragraphs from the book in a play. The play's producers offered to pay a substantial fee for permission, but the rights owners simply refused. They were entitled to do this; as rights owners they are entitled to refuse to authorize any restricted act carried out on their work. Because of the importance of the two paragraphs, which were, they argued, core to the theme of the book, the two paragraphs would be a 'substantial' part of the work.

The *adaptation right* covers actions such as translations, converting a dramatic work to a non-dramatic work and vice versa, conversion into a strip cartoon, and arrangements or transcriptions of musical works. Many actions that might appear to be an adaptation, such as taking a work and changing the spelling from American English into English English, are in fact acts of copying rather than adaptation. It makes little difference – it is still a restricted act! The person who has made the adaptation may well have copyright in the adapted work, as they have used skill and effort to create the new work, but without the permission of the owner of the copyright in the original work, they cannot perform any restricted act with their new work.

WEB 2.0 POINT

Web 2.0 applications may well incorporate such adaptations, so there is a real risk of infringement.

The *communication to the public right* is especially important in Web 2.0 applications. The copyright owner's permission is required before a third party can send a copyright work to others using telecommunications. Thus, the placing of an item on a website, as an e-mail attachment or on an intranet, or broadcasting the work are all examples of communication to the public (and once again, the public includes any sub-set of the public). It is important to note that it makes no difference whether any third party has viewed the copyright work so transmitted – only that they had the ability to do so if they so wished.

WEB 2.0 POINT

All Web 2.0 activities by definition involve communicating to the public the content of the service or application. Thus, permission is required if there is any third party content held within the Web 2.0 service. While any user-generated content is probably fine because by submitting something to the wiki, blog and so on the user has implicitly granted permission for the material to be communicated to the public, the same is not true of third party materials, such as music, images, films, sound recordings or texts not created by the user submitting that content.

Infringement

Copyright infringement occurs when someone undertakes one (or more) of these restricted acts without the permission of the copyright owner. However, as we shall see, there are circumstances where the law allows people to undertake acts that would otherwise be infringement (see the section 'Exceptions to copyright' below). For infringement to have occurred, the infringing act must have taken place on all or a substantial part of the original work – but as we have seen, 'substantial' simply means 'important', rather than 'the majority'.

Exercise 4

Jo has digitized one chapter from an in copyright book for putting into a wiki. She has been told this is OK because the law allows one to copy one chapter of a book or a single article from a journal issue. Is Jo safe from an infringement action?

There are various ways one can infringe. First, one can simply perform one or more of the restricted acts without permission. Second, one can 'authorize infringement', either by directly instructing someone to carry out an infringing act, or by running an organization in such a way that a blind eye is turned to infringements that are regularly occurring.

Case study L

Most publishers require the author of a manuscript submitted to them to warrant that the material submitted does not infringe any third party copyright, and is not illegal in any way (for example, defamatory). This is a reasonable thing to request. However, some publishers go further and insist that the author provides evidence that they have received formal permission from rights holders for reproducing any third party material, irrespective of the length of the material copied (as it may be insubstantial), or irrespective of the fact that the copying is under a *bona fide* exception (in particular, criticism or review – see below). This causes significant problems for authors. The publishers are being unnecessarily cautious. This is an example of how a failure to understand copyright law properly leads to the slowing down or prevention of worthwhile publications.

The usual consequence of infringement is a civil court action, where the copyright owner sues for damages. The damages requested may be based on the lost sales that the rights owner has suffered, or the money made (or saved) by the infringer by their actions – the rights owner can decide which approach they want to take when pursuing the action. Other penalties could include delivery up (the requirement that the infringer passes all the infringing copies in its possession to the rights owner) or destruction of the infringing items, and/or a court order forbidding any future infringement (and if that order were ignored, the infringer would be in contempt of court). Only rarely does infringement result in criminal proceedings –in cases of piracy (selling infringing goods) and a few other obviously criminal activities. Claims by some rights holder organizations, such as the Federation Against Copyright Theft, that copyright infringement is (by implication always) a criminal activity are misleading. In most infringement cases, criminal proceedings are not possible.

Infringement of digital materials is a particular concern for rights owners. This is because it is simple to copy an electronic work, the copy so made is typically very high quality, the copies can be easily disseminated to a very large number of other people, the costs of copying are trivial, and it is very difficult to police what uploading and downloading is occurring. It is therefore not surprising that rights owners, especially those in the music, film and software sectors, are so vigorous in their attempts to restrict illegal copying of digital materials. The section 'Recent changes to the law' shows how they have been partly successful in achieving their objectives.

WEB 2.0 POINT
The risks of infringement in a Web 2.0 product are high. Readers who are concerned about the legal issues associated with Web 2.0, and would like advice on policies, template requests for permission as well as a diagnostic tool to identify risks combined with risk management advice, should consult the web2rights website at www.web2rights.org.uk.

Some examples: Don't put somebody else's images up on Flickr unless you have permission from the rights owner. Putting items up on Flickr under an 'All Rights Reserved' licence/notice will not damage your ability to license them commercially for profit subsequently. However, the Flickr licence gives it permission to use the images for displaying, distributing and promoting the Flickr service; for anything else they must respect your copyright or licence.

Legal ways of making copies

Notwithstanding the apparently onerous restrictions placed on users of copyright materials, there are a number of ways to undertake restricted acts on all or a substantial part of copyright works without having to worry about falling foul of the law. There are three ways:

1. Take advantage of one or more of the so-called 'exceptions to copyright' provided in the law.
2. Make use of materials where the rights owner has explicitly granted free permission to use the materials or has explicitly waived copyright.
3. Buy a licence from the copyright owner or someone authorized to act on behalf of the copyright owner.

Exceptions to copyright

This is a generic term for all those actions, that are explicitly permitted under the CDPA. The reason for these exceptions is that governments have recognized that to grant a total monopoly to rights holders would not be in the public interest, as much social, economic and educational benefit is derived from exploitation of copyright works. Incidentally, the wording in the CDPA refers to 'acts permitted in relation to copyright works'; but people typically refer to these provisions as 'exceptions', 'permitted acts', 'private copying' or 'exemptions'. It is misleading, however, to describe them as 'user rights', because all the exceptions are *defences against an infringement action* rather than fundamental user rights – at least that is how UK law stands at the moment. These exceptions are compatible with the UK's international commitments under the Berne Convention, TRIPS and relevant EU directives. All the international conventions allow exceptions to copyright under certain restricted circumstances.

Sections 28–76 of the CDPA describe the numerous exceptions to copyright that are allowed for under the law. The fact that there are nearly 50 such sections demonstrates just how varied and complex the exceptions regime is in the UK. However, it should be stressed that the vast majority of these exceptions are of little relevance to Web 2.0 applications, or indeed to library and information managers. So while the focus here is on the few that might be relevant, it is worth checking the CDPA itself, or relevant textbooks, to find out whether a particular use of a copyright work might be subject of an exception.

Probably the best known, but also, unfortunately, one of the most widely misunderstood, exception is 'fair dealing'. *Fair dealing* allows an individual to make one – or more under some circumstances – copies of all or a substantial part of a copyright work (one doesn't need to invoke the defence of fair dealing or of any other exception to copyright if an insubstantial part of a work is being copied, because that by definition cannot be infringement), without having to ask permission or pay fees, so long as certain conditions apply. These conditions relate to the purpose of the copying and whether it is fair or not. Only three purposes are allowed in UK law; it should be noted that some other countries' laws provide much more generous permitted purposes. The three permitted purposes in the UK are non-commercial research or private study, reporting current events, and criticism or review. The concept of non-commercial research or private study causes some difficulty in interpretation, but it is reasonable to assume that research undertaken with an explicit commercial purpose, such as that undertaken by a pharmaceutical company, is commercial, and therefore outside this exception, while purely scholarly research is likely to be non-commercial, and so is acceptable. But there are grey areas, such as research carried out for the purpose of preparing for an interview, which, if successful, will lead to promotion and increased pay. It is not clear whether that is commercial research or not. This is just one of the many areas of copyright law where ambiguity rules.

Reporting current events is somewhat more straightforward. One can copy a copyright work for the purpose of reporting something, which is in the news. A common-sense approach would be that if this were the sort of thing that would appear in a broadcast news bulletin or newspaper, it is acceptable to copy material for this purpose. Criticism or review refers not just to book or film reviews, where it is acceptable to copy material to emphasize the points being made, but it is also acceptable to copy something from source A in order to criticize or review item B. While the courts have interpreted this exception rather broadly, it should be emphasized that merely adding, say, some background music or images to a presentation that is criticizing something else is not acceptable if the purpose is simply making the presentation more interesting or pleasant.

One of the common misunderstandings about the fair dealing exception is that if the purpose falls within the definitions the law provides for, then all is OK. It is not. There is a second, equally important criterion. The copying must be fair: it must not damage the legitimate commercial or other interests of the rights owner.

There is also a myth that copying one chapter of a book or one article from a journal is always 'fair'. It is not necessarily so; each case would have to be examined on its merits by a court.

Exercise 5

Angela uploads onto her blog a scanned image of a commercially published street map in order to criticize it because it does not show a key geographic feature. Would she be able to justify this under fair dealing?

The important thing to remember about fair dealing is that it must pass *both* these tests (purpose and not damaging the rights owner's interests) to be acceptable. Even then, it must be stressed that it is simply a defence against an infringement action, and if sued one would have to demonstrate that the material was indeed copied for one of the permitted purposes, and that it did not damage the legitimate interests of the copyright owner.

Fair dealing is not the only potentially useful exception to copyright. There are others for librarians and archivists (the library privilege defence, not considered in detail here; interested readers should read one of the standard texts for library and information staff for more details on it), and for those with visual impairments. There are also important exceptions for the *setting and answering of formal examinations* that will be of use to both teachers and their students, and a useful exception for those involved in *legal cases* (the judicial proceedings exception). Many *public administration* functions are provided for with exceptions, and there are very specific and rather limited exceptions applying to teaching, computer programs, artists' works for sale, so-called author abstracts in scholarly journals, and databases. Finally, there is an interesting exception allowing copying if it is *in the public interest*, though courts have interpreted that exception very narrowly so far.

It is important to note that some of the exceptions to copyright apply to some but not all media types, and some do not extend to all the restricted acts, so anyone planning to copy an in copyright work needs to assure themselves that not only is the purpose acceptable, but also that the exception does indeed apply to the particular media type in question and that it covers the proposed restricted acts involved.

WEB 2.0 POINT

Very few of the exceptions to copyright apply to Web 2.0 applications. Some fair dealing exceptions might be justified when one considers the purpose of copying, but because Web 2.0 applications tend to have a wide readership, they are unlikely to be fair. Very rarely will the other exceptions apply to a Web 2.0 application.

Explicit waivers of copyright and free licences

Naturally, if the copyright owner has explicitly stated that they are choosing not to exercise copyright, that material can be copied. This approach is less common than the granting of a free of charge licence to copy. The most popular type of this approach is the use of a Creative Commons licence. Details about Creative Commons can be found at http://creativecommons.org. In essence, a Creative Commons licence is voluntarily applied to any electronic material – text, images, moving images, sound recordings and the like by the rights owner. There is a family of about six different licences that can be used, but they all have one thing in common – the rights owner is stating that any third party is free to copy and further disseminate the material, so long as the rights owner is acknowledged. There might be further restrictions, e.g. it must not be used to make money, or the material has to be used 'as is', and should not be amended (including taking extracts) or merged with other material. Much of the material on Web 2.0 sites does indeed include a proportion of Creative Commons licensed materials, e.g. Flickr and YouTube. Other Web 2.0 services may well comprise only Creative Commons materials. Both Yahoo! and Google allow a searcher to restrict their search to only Creative Commons licensed materials. The UK Government is also generous with its free licences to copy and re-disseminate its publications.

It is often assumed that it is acceptable (there is a free of charge implied licence) to copy anything available for free on the web. The concept of implied licences needs, however, to be thought through carefully. While it is reasonable to assume that a person placed material on the web with the express intention that others should *link* to it, it is not always the case that the rights owner will be happy that the material has been *copied*. One should always put oneself in the position of the rights owner, and ask whether that person might be upset if their material was used in the particular application in question. If there are any doubts on this matter, one should approach the rights owner for formal permission.

Purchased licences

Many readers will be familiar with the concept of paid-for licences. Individual publishers, TV companies, film organizations, collective licensing bodies such as the Copyright Licensing Agency, and online hosts and aggregators offer them. The principles behind all these licences are the same; the licences state that, notwithstanding the strictures of the CDPA, the licensor (the copyright owner or someone acting on its behalf) grants the licensee (the person paying for the licence) permission to carry out certain restricted acts, so long as the ground rules of the licence terms are followed and agreed fees are paid. Very often the licence also provides an indemnity, so the licensee is assured that there is no risk that they will be sued for copyright infringement as long as they follow the terms of the licence.

WEB 2.0 POINT

One needs to check the terms of the licence carefully to make sure the uses made of the work in a Web 2.0 application are indeed permitted under the terms of the licence. Many licences currently on offer take no account of Web 2.0 and it may be worth negotiating the terms of such licences to ensure that they permit the copying of the materials into a Web 2.0 application, and for the subsequent re-use or dissemination of the copied materials within a Web 2.0 environment.

Anyone who submits material to a Web 2.0 service will normally not be assigning (giving away) their copyright, but will be granting the Web 2.0 service a (normally free) licence to reproduce the materials submitted. Anyone who submits materials to a Web 2.0 service should double-check that they are not committing to anything more than that.

Orphan works

Orphan works are a large and growing problem. An orphan work is a work that is in copyright, but the rights owner cannot be identified or traced, so there is no one to approach for permission to carry out a restricted act on the work. It has always been a problem, but that problem is increasingly significantly as the amount of material available on the web but without an identifiable owner has grown. While it is of particular concern to those libraries and archives that wish to undertake mass digitization projects covering all their holdings, it is also a problem for anyone else seeking permission to reproduce something.

The law as it currently stands does not provide much help. Any restricted act on the work is potentially infringing if one has not received permission from the owner and if it does not fall under one or more of the exceptions to copyright noted earlier. The fact that one had made strenuous efforts to track down and identify the owner is irrelevant in the law. A number of possible solutions to the problem can be identified, including the introduction of a new exception to copyright for such works, or a compulsory licensing scheme of some type. The UK Government introduced a licensing scheme in the Digital Economy Bill in 2010, but the particular clause was dropped because of strong opposition by the photographers' lobby. The Hargreaves Review of UK copyright law (see below) recommended a similar type of licensing scheme, and the Government has said it supports this idea. The full text of the Review can be found at www.ipo.gov.uk/ipreview-finalreport.pdf. Time will tell if such a scheme is implemented. Nonetheless, there continue to be discussions in the UK and the EU about changes to the law to address the problem, and it is likely the law will become more flexible regarding orphan works sooner or later.

Recent changes to the law

Over the years since the passage of the CDPA there have been changes to the law. These changes are ongoing and at the time of writing (mid 2012) some were in the pipeline. It should be noted that this part of the chapter may be out of date by the time the book is read, and readers are urged to check the latest situation from the UK Intellectual Property Office's website (www.ipo.gov.uk).

Apart from the introduction of a new exception for the visually impaired, the changes to copyright law in the UK in recent years have been in one direction – to make copyright law more favourable to rights owners. Examples include the extension of the lifetime of most copyright works from life + 50 years to life + 70 years, the introduction of new database rights (discussed in Chapter 3), increased penalties for criminal infringements, and explicit legal protection for technical protection methods (TPMs) and rights management information (discussed below). Some readers may be aware of the Hargreaves Review of copyright law. Its recommendations were published in summer 2011, and the Government accepted all of them. However, some of the proposed changes to the law are controversial with rights owners. This book reports the current state of play, but readers are urged to keep themselves up to date in case of further changes in the near future.

There was another important change to the law when the 2010 Digital Economy Act came into force. Among its provisions was a 'three strikes and you are out' law, which would mean that if a rights holder found evidence of copyright infringement, he or she was entitled to demand, through the relevant internet service provider, that the subscriber cease such activity. If the subscriber continued to upload or download materials illegally, a second warning would be sent. If this, too, were ignored, then the ISP would be required to reduce or cut off altogether the subscriber's connection. At the time this book was written, these contentious clauses were on the statute book, but had not yet been implemented.

TPMs have also benefited from changes to the law. They are any technical device (such as an ID or password system) that prevents non-authorized users from accessing copyright materials. Until recently, it was not an offence to bypass them in order to infringe, but this is no longer the case. The law was changed so that it is now an offence knowingly to bypass or disable a TPM with a view to infringing, or concealing an infringement of copyright. However, this raises the question of what happens if someone needs to access some material hidden behind a TPM but for *bona fide* purposes, for example, for criticism or review? In theory, the law provides a mechanism whereby the person wishing to do so contacts the rights holder, and if permission is refused, the user can make a complaint to the relevant government minister, and the minister investigates. If the minister agrees that the TPM should be lowered on this occasion, and tells the rights owner accordingly, but the rights owner still refuses to co-operate, the user has the right to sue the rights owner. However, this procedure is so cumbersome (and is much more cumbersome than in other countries that have similar legislation) that no one has availed themselves of the procedure. Nonetheless, the position for users in the USA is worse, as there is no procedure at all built in to the law for appealing against an unjustified TPM.

The way the law has been implemented serves to emphasize the fact that exceptions to copyright are *not* regarded in UK law as user *rights*, but as defences against an infringement action, though as an aside it is worth noting that the World Intellectual Property Organization (WIPO) is considering making library and archive exceptions to copyright rights for those organizations. Incidentally, many people confuse TPMs with so-called digital rights management systems (DRMSs). A TPM is just one (final) component within a DRMS. DRMSs cover the entire 'lifecycle' of digital rights, from working out and then identifying who the rights owner is, via communicating who the rights owner is (see rights management information below), via declaring terms and conditions for use, all the way through to enforcing protection of those rights – TPMs.

Rights management information refers to any information associated with a copyright work that identifies who the rights owner is. An example would be '© Charles Oppenheim 2012'. Recent changes to the law made it an offence to delete or amend any rights management information with a view to infringing, or concealing an infringement. Surprisingly enough, before this change of the law, it appears there was no explicit legal protection against such abuse of rights management information.

Differences between UK and US copyright law
Because of their common adherence to the Berne Convention and the Universal Copyright Convention, the fundamentals of the laws of the USA and the UK are the same. However, there are some important differences, as shown in Figure 2.1.

A copyright checklist
Readers developing a Web 2.0 application might find the checklist in Figure 2.2, adapted from the Web2Rights website (www.web2rights.org.uk) helpful.

Another useful resource, covering not just copyright, but also data protection and other legal issues, can be found at www.jisclegal.ac.uk/ManageContent/ManageContent/tabid/243/ID/2115/Facing-up-to-Facebook-A-Guide-for-FE-and-HE-HTML.aspx. Although aimed at educational users of Facebook, in practice the advice given is generally applicable to all Web 2.0 applications.

1. The major exception to copyright in US law is known as 'fair use' rather than 'fair dealing', but the difference is not just a cosmetic one of name. In the UK, 'fair dealing' is strictly defined by purpose – only certain purposes qualify and copying for any other purpose is not allowed. In contrast, 'fair use' is not constrained by purpose but simply provides broad criteria for what would be acceptable practice. There are pros and cons to both approaches. The UK law provides some level of certainty, so the number of court cases relating to it is small, but is regarded by many users as too restrictive. US law is far more flexible, but this gives more scope for disagreement, and so the number of court cases involving fair use is large.
2. US law regarding copying for teaching purposes is more generous than UK law.
3. US law regarding copying digital materials for preservation or archiving is also more generous than UK law.
4. On the other hand, as noted above, US law on TPMs is somewhat more rigid than UK law.
5. Also as noted above, US law is somewhat more bureaucratic as it requires a rights owner to register their copyright if they intend to start infringement proceedings in a US court. There is no such formality in the UK.
6. The rules on the lifetime of copyright in the USA are more complex than those in the UK.

Figure 2.1 *Differences between UK and US copyright law*

- Have you prepared:
— a step-by-step plan of what your project is about?
— what you want to achieve?
— in what ways the project outputs will be accessible and usable over the shorter and longer term?
- Have you considered any funding conditions and how these are to be complied with when developing your copyright strategy?
- Have you identified all the different types of technology, services, software and content you will be developing, using and accessing?
- Have you identified all the different types of uses you and your users will make of the technology, services, software and content?

Figure 2.2 *A copyright checklist*   *(continued on next page)*

- Have you identified all the authors and owners of copyright who will be contributing to the development of the technology, services, software and the content as part of your project?
- Have you identified all of the third party content you wish to use and access, decided what you want to use it for and whether you need to seek permission?
- Are you comfortable that the elements of the strategy mesh will enable you and your target audience to use the technology, services, software and content in the way you wish over the shorter and longer term?
- If you are using third party content without permission (or if works infringing content might be placed on your technology, services or software by your users or any other third party) have you considered the level of the risk?
- Have you thought about developing a notice and take down policy?
- Have you investigated professional indemnity insurance?
- Is your project one that is suitable to be made available to a limited audience from behind technological protection controls?

Figure 2.2 *Continued*

Conclusions

This chapter has only touched on the major aspects of UK copyright law, including the nature of copyright, its lifetime, the restricted acts and infringement, how to avoid infringement, and recent developments in the law, highlighting the implications for those involved in Web 2.0. Readers are strongly advised to check more detailed textbooks for particular aspects of the law. An annotated list of some useful resources is provided in Chapter 9.

It is also worth stressing again that the law is under constant review, and that changes to copyright law are threatened (if that is the right word) by both the UK Government and the EU. There is a sense of polarization in the world of copyright between those who represent rights holders (especially those who earn substantial income from copyright, such as the music, publishing, film, software and computer games industries) and users of information. This is especially true in electronic information, where an entire generation has grown up used to the concept of being able to download materials for free from the internet – a generation that often criticizes the copyright industries for their alleged excessive profits and out of date business models. This tension can be seen in the extremely different views expressed by representatives of both sides in submissions to the numerous reviews and inquiries into copyright law that have plagued the UK recently. Government's role is to ensure the law continues to encourage investment in the copyright industries, while at the same time satisfying the legitimate demands of users for acceptable levels of access and use of copyright materials. Until recently, it seemed that Government listened only to the rights owners, but this may be coming to an end. A law weighted too far in favour of rights owners might lead to refusal by large numbers to abide by the ground rules the law lays down. Whatever way this tension plays out, one thing remains true: unfortunately, the rule for those involved in copyright is the same as for everyone involved in legal matters – ignorance of the law is no excuse. The onus is on readers to keep themselves up to date.

Answers to exercises
Exercise 1
This is not an uncommon situation. As carrying out teaching is part of the employee's duties, the default legal position is that the copyright in all the teaching materials belongs to the employer. Therefore, in principle, Fred cannot take the materials with him when he changes jobs. However, the college would benefit from recruiting a new lecturer with a ready-made collection of teaching materials, and this should be balanced against the formal legal position. Thus, most colleges turn a blind eye to the practice of a departing lecturer taking their teaching materials with them. The best approach is that when Fred leaves he is given a licence by his ex-employer to use the materials created by him in any future employment. Thus Fred is free to continue his trade in his new post. In the meantime, the college will gain the benefit of an incoming replacement lecturer, who can hit the ground running, so to speak, because they have permission from their last employer to exploit teaching materials they created in the past.

Exercise 2
Copyright in all George Orwell's published works will expire on 31 December 2020. As copyright lifetime is tied to the lifetime of the creator, it makes no difference who owns the copyright right now. From 1 January 2021, anyone can reproduce any of George Orwell's words without having to ask permission.

Exercise 3
Yes, this is substantial because this is the crucial line of the book – it tells the reader who the murderer was, and reproducing it elsewhere could well damage sales of the book.

Exercise 4
No, Jo is not necessarily safe. It is a common myth that it is always OK to copy one chapter from a book or one article from a journal. This is because people confuse library privilege permissions with general permissions. In reality, it would

all depend on whether what had been scanned was considered substantial or not, and each case is decided on its merits.

Exercise 5

While there is a strong case for arguing this is indeed being reproduced for the purposes of criticism or review, it may still be outside the exception because the reproduction of the map damages the sales of the map to potential purchasers, who can obtain the map from Angela's blog at no cost instead.

CHAPTER 3

Other intellectual property rights and related rights

Introduction

Copyright is not the only type of IPR that someone running, or contributing to, a Web 2.0 service needs to be aware of. There are a large number of other types of IPR they might encounter, such as database right, moral rights, performers' rights, trademarks or domain names and patents. This chapter considers each of them, outlining some of the pitfalls that Web 2.0 users might fall into.

Database rights

In normal everyday usage, a database might be defined as 'a large collection of data, works and other elements stored electronically', but the formal legal definition in the CDPA is somewhat different. It defines a database as 'a collection of independent works, data or other materials arranged in a systematic or methodical way and individually accessible by electronic or other means'. There are two key differences between the common-sense definition and the formal legal definition. The first is that that the database does not have to be electronic – it could be a collection of printed items or photographs, and so on. The second is that the word 'large' does not appear, so even a very modest collection of (say) a dozen items could be considered a database in law. The two definitions do have one thing in common though – there is no requirement in either definition that each individual item enjoys copyright or any other kind of IPR in its own right.

Exercise 1

Which of the following would be considered to be a database in law?

- the personal library of someone, comprising books and magazines
- a university library online catalogue
- a collection of First World War poems
- a list of shorthand nicknames for, and full e-mail addresses of, contacts, as held by a regular e-mail user
- an e-mail thread comprising various contributions, some lengthy and some not, from various individuals

- someone's bank statement
- a list of the melting points of a few dozen inorganic compounds
- a collection of postings on Facebook
- a single document built up by several contributor individuals on a wiki.

In UK law, as in other EU member states, databases can be protected in one or both of two ways. They may be protected by copyright as literary works, and/or database rights may protect them. There is also a group of databases that enjoy no protection at all, as we shall see.

To enjoy copyright protection as a *literary work*, first the database must be original – not copied from somewhere else – and it must show some level of creativity by reason of the selection or arrangement of the contents of the database. This makes databases unusual in the group of items considered to be literary works in UK copyright law, because there is no such requirement for creativity for other literary works. This sort of requirement of intellectual creativity is common in the copyright laws of continental European countries, and arguably the fact that such wording was agreed by the UK in the passage of the EU directive on databases demonstrates a willingness by the UK to consider some sort of compromise between the UK copyright law tradition of 'sweat of the brow' and the European tradition of creativity. As with the rest of literary works, the author is the person who created the database. If, as is often the case, the database is created by a team of individuals working under a contract of employment, then the employer is normally the owner of the resulting database. Note that a database can be a literary work, but not an artistic work or any of the other standard types of copyright work. Thus, a collection of artistic works, sound recordings, TV programmes and so on cannot enjoy copyright in the collection, though they can enjoy database right (see below).

WEB 2.0 POINT

A folksonomy might enjoy copyright in the database of tagging elements that has been built up by a number of contributors.

To enjoy *database right*, the rules are more relaxed. First, the collection can be of multiple works in any medium, not just of words and numbers (though the law is worded so that an individual film, TV programme and so on cannot in law be a database, and nor can a CD comprising several music tracks). Second, there is no requirement for any creativity, as required for databases to be literary works (see above). Instead, to enjoy database right, there must have been 'substantial investment in obtaining, verifying or presenting the contents of the database'. The key issue at stake here, as identified in some major European Court of Justice decisions, is that this definition does *not* include substantial investment in *creating the raw data* in the first place. Thus, irrespective of how much effort went into the research that led to the data being made, if the database fails the above criteria, it cannot get database right. It is fair to say that the vast majority of commentators were astonished when the European Court decided that the initial making of the data could not be considered when evaluating whether or not a database is entitled to database right protection. Thus, the substantial investment refers to the resources expended to seek out pre-existing data and/or verifying their accuracy and/or collating and then presenting them, but does not extend to the primary creation of the contents of the database itself.

WEB 2.0 POINT

It is not clear if a folksonomy would enjoy database right under these criteria.

Case study A

EUROPEAN COURT OF JUSTICE CASE – BRITISH HORSERACING BOARD LTD V. WILLIAM HILL ORGANISATION LTD.

This case was decided in 2005. British Horseracing Board Ltd (BHB) sued William Hill Ltd, the well known firm of bookmakers, for using parts of its database of horses and jockeys who were going to race in future races without paying a licence fee. There was no claim of copyright infringement, as the BHB acknowledged implicitly that there had been no intellectual creativity involved in making the master database – it was simply a comprehensive database of runners, jockeys, owners and so on. The case was about infringement of database right only. The Court decided (as noted above, to much surprise) there was no database right in these details because the Board had already created the database for quite different purposes (the general management of UK horse-racing), and no particular resource had gone into the obtaining, verification or display of the contents of the database that it was licensing to other bookmakers for a fee. In future, therefore, courts in the EU must decide how much effort went into the obtaining and verification of data that had been collected previously for possibly a quite different purpose. That will not be an easy task, and it is likely that courts in different member states will adopt different approaches to this question. One result of this case will be that organizations that sell databases within the EU will make significant resources available to obtain, verify and display data they offer for licence (and will keep a record of those efforts), and/or will make efforts to only offer selections from a master database they might hold, and thereby gain copyright protection for their databases as literary works on the grounds that intellectual effort was used to decide what would go in the database and what would not.

To enjoy database right, significant effort must have been expended on things other than the creation of the original data and, arguably, a database that just happens to spin out of some other activity will not enjoy database rights. The owner of database right is the 'person' (a legal term, which covers both individuals and organizations) that takes the initiative in obtaining, verifying or presenting the contents of the database, and assumes the financial risk involved.

The rights enjoyed by the rights owners

It is worth pausing here to consider where we have reached. To enjoy copyright protection, a database must be a literary work, and must involve the author's own intellectual creativity. In contrast, to enjoy database right, there must have been significant expenditure or resources spent on obtaining, verifying or presenting the data, irrespective of any resources expended in the initial creation of the data. There will be databases that enjoy no rights at all, for example, one that comprises an obvious comprehensive list, and which have not involved significant resources spent on obtaining, verifying or presenting. A small-scale example is a person's Christmas card list; a larger-scale example is a White Pages telephone directory in alphabetical order of surname.

Exercise 2

Which of the databases in Exercise 1 are likely to enjoy copyright? Which database right? Which no rights at all?

If the database is a literary work, the standard lifetime rules apply (70 years from the death of the author, or, if it is an anonymous database, or one owned by a corporate organization, 70 years from the data of first publication), as do the standard rules about the rights enjoyed and exceptions to those rights. If the database enjoys database right, the right lasts for 15 years from the end of the year when the database was created, or from the data when it was first published, whichever is the later. If the database is subjected to significant changes over that 15-year period, then the 15-year period gets renewed, in principle indefinitely so long as significant changes are made. At the time of writing this book, in 2012, database right as an IPR was under 15 years old, so no test of the renewability has been considered. The list of infringing acts for a database is shorter than for copyright. The only way to infringe is to extract and/or re-utilize all or a substantial part of the database by a single or repeated set of actions. A lawful user can *always* extract or re-utilize insubstantial parts, even if a contract purports to prevent that. In addition, there is a permitted act for anyone, which is to extract material from a database 'for the purpose of illustration for teaching or research' for a non-commercial purpose, so long as the source is indicated. The meanings of the weasel word 'illustration', which comes straight from the EU directive, is completely obscure, and there have been no test cases to provide a meaning. It is interesting to note that there is no fair dealing defence for copyright works in UK law for teaching purposes, but there is this one for database right. Of course, if the database right has expired, anyone can do what they like with it – so long, of course, as there are no works in copyright being copied, whether individual components of the database, or the database as a whole. Thus, any re-use of an old database is only safe once one has checked the copyright status of the database as a whole, and of its individual components.

Database right and copyright in a database are not mutually exclusive. It is possible for a database to enjoy just copyright, just database right, both or none. In the case where a database has copyright as a literary work, the standard rules of copyright apply. This is helpful because the rights granted to a copyright owner are more extensive than those granted to a database right owner, and the ground rules of copyright are often more familiar to creators than database rights. In the case of database rights, it is important to remember that to enjoy these rights the test imposed by the European Court about significant expenditure of resources or money in obtaining, verifying and presenting the contents must apply.

WEB 2.0 POINT

Databases are almost certain to arise in all kinds of Web 2.0 applications. Thus, for example, a slide share collection, or a collection of videos, may well enjoy database rights. Similarly, a wiki comprising a series of contributions from different participants is likely to enjoy database rights and may well also be subject to copyright. As noted above, a folksonomy may well enjoy copyright, but is less likely to be protected by database rights.

Users of Web 2.0 applications should make themselves familiar with the rights that might be enjoyed by third parties in any database they copy or re-use.

It should be noted that while the law in most EU member states is virtually uniform on database rights, which is hardly surprising considering all their laws derive from an EU directive on the topic, in the USA databases are not explicitly protected in law. Many databases enjoy copyright in the USA, but, following a US court decision in the 1990s, databases such as a White Pages telephone directory, comprising as they do simple facts arranged in an 'obvious' way (alphabetical order of surname) do not have any protection.

Case study B

FEIST PUBLICATIONS INC. V. RURAL TELEPHONE SERVICE CO.
This 1991 US Supreme Court decision followed action by Rural, which objected to Feist taking substantial portions of one of its White Pages

telephone directories and incorporating it into a Feist publication. The Supreme Court decided that copyright protection was not available to such a directory, as to enjoy copyright a work should display at least a modicum of creativity. The Supreme Court held that mere sweat of the brow was not enough, but made it clear that a bare minimum of creativity was enough to get the work protection under US copyright law. The Court argued there had been no selectivity involved, as all telephone subscribers were listed, and that organizing the surnames alphabetically was commonplace and involved no creativity. (As an aside, in Iceland, where the number of surnames used by the population is very low, the standard telephone directory is in alphabetical order of subscribers' first names.) Thus, in the USA, simple directories with entries arranged in an obvious manner do not enjoy any protection at all, as US law does not at present have a law explicitly protecting databases. However, it must be stressed that in practice very few databases fail to be protected in the USA, as the majority involve a modicum of selection or arrangement in a non-obvious manner.

It was possibly in response to this nominal weakening of the law in the USA that the EU worked on its Database Directive, hoping thereby to encourage the development of EU-based databases with their database right protection. If that was the EU's primary motivation, it was based on an incorrect premise, as all the evidence suggests that in recent years the USA has developed many more successful databases than EU member states have. My own assessment is that the laws in the EU and the USA are, in practice, not that far apart, and the reason for the continued success of US database producers is more to do with entrepreneurial skills and willingness by those with money to invest in risky ventures than the legal background.

WEB 2.0 POINT

Anyone submitting materials to a Web 2.0 service will probably be granting the service a licence to reproduce what is submitted. They may also be explicitly granting the Web 2.0 service copyright and/or database rights in their contributions to the service.

Moral rights

Moral rights are separate from other IPRs, despite the fact that in the UK they are covered by the CDPA, which also governs copyright and database rights law. Moral rights are based on continental European ideas relating to copyright, whereby the rights of the individual creator are considered to be as or even more important as any economic rights the rights owner may hold. As part of its obligations under the various international copyright treaties it is a signatory to, the UK adopted some limited moral rights for creators in the 1988 Act. The three main moral rights granted to individuals are paternity right, the right to object to derogatory treatment and the right of false attribution.

Paternity right is the right of a creator to have him or herself identified as the creator (author or director) of a copyright work. This right has to be *asserted* in writing – in other words, it is not automatic. While this is arguably in breach of the UK's international obligations, no one has made a legal challenge to this particular quirk of the law. In a further limitation in UK law, reflecting no doubt the Government's lack of enthusiasm for the foreign idea of authors' rights, the right is not available to the design of a typeface; to a publication in a newspaper, magazine or other periodical; or to text in an encyclopaedia, dictionary or other collective work of reference. Again, arguably this is contrary to the UK's international obligations, but remains on the statute book.

The *right to object to derogatory treatment* – the so-called integrity right – does not need to be asserted in advance. This gives the creator the right to object if a third party makes any amendment to a copyright work that damages the reputation of the creator, and then publishes the amended work in any way. This would apply, for example, to quoting a third party out of context, or deliberately changing their use of words or images to suggest something about them that is unfair. Similar limitations to the applicability of this right to certain works as for paternity rights apply.

The *right of false attribution* gives any person, whether a creator or not, the right to object if something they did not create has their name associated with it. This has the effect of curbing some of the excesses of tabloid journalists, who sometimes put words into the mouth of someone when that person did not record such words.

There is also another (so-called) moral right relating to the use of photographs or films of individuals commissioned from a third party. The person who did the commissioning has under some circumstances the right to prevent publication or display of those images, even though it is the photographer or filmmaker who owns the copyright. This is really a right more to do with privacy than to do with moral rights.

Performers also enjoy some of the above moral rights in their performances.

Other than derogatory treatment, these rights last as long as the copyright in the work. Derogatory treatment right lasts for 20 years after the death of the creator (presumably their heirs and successors would take up the cudgels on their behalf). If any of the moral rights are infringed, the aggrieved party can sue for damages. Certain exceptions to copyright, if used by a third party (for example, fair dealing), may make the third party exempt from accusations of infringement of moral rights. A key point to make is that, unlike copyright or database right, moral rights cannot be assigned to a third party – they remain with the creator forever. They can, however, be waived, and indeed some contracts, for example, between authors and publishers, may *require* the author to waive some or all of their moral rights. This, too, is different from continental Europe, where, in general, moral rights can never be waived. Waivers are helpful for those who publish works because they allow them to make minor adjustments without having to seek the consent of the creator.

WEB 2.0 POINT

Under UK law, contributors to services such as Wikipedia have no right to be identified as the authors. The same applies to any jointly authored reference work, however that term might be interpreted. For other Web 2.0 applications, if the contributor wishes to be identified as the author, they need to make a public statement asserting their right. Few do so in practice. The informality of many Web 2.0 applications means that derogatory treatment of a work is likely to occur. Thus, for example, in a discussion thread, a third party may deliberately quote a previous contributor out of context in order to ridicule their views. There are risks, too, that the right to object to one's name being associated with something that the person did not create may occur in some Web 2.0 applications.

At the same time, one must be careful not to infringe third party rights when using third party materials within a Web 2.0 application. Thus, correct attribution of sources – something that is good practice in any case – is in fact required by law in the case of the use of third party copyright works where the author is clearly identified. Similarly, one should not quote out of context, or attribute things to someone who did not create the item in question. Problems associated with moral rights can become particularly acute when mashups are created.

Exercise 3

Are any moral rights being infringed by the following actions?

1. I reproduce a scholarly journal article by Professor Peabody in a wiki, but fail to attribute it to him and instead pretend I wrote it.
2. I use selections from a folksonomy developed by a large team of contributors to critique the approach used by the developers of the structure of that folksonomy.
3. I incorporate part of a Cliff Richard record into a mashup of sounds I have developed on a YouTube recording I have posted without naming him.
4. I claim that Professor Peabody has issued a statement supporting my point of view on a contentious topic without checking whether he has made such a statement or not.

WEB 2.0 POINT
Anyone submitting materials to a Web 2.0 service should check that any licence they are agreeing to covers any moral rights; for example, they should be able to assert their moral right of paternity if they feel they wish to.

The concept of moral rights is not formally developed in US law. Copyright law in the USA emphasizes protection of financial reward over protection of creative attribution. When the USA signed the Berne Convention, it claimed that the Convention's moral rights provisions were addressed sufficiently by other statutes, such as defamation laws. However, this argument is disingenuous. Some individual states have moral rights laws, particularly pertaining to visual art and artists. Monty Python famously managed to rely on moral rights in 1975 in its proceedings against an American TV network for airing re-edited versions of its TV series. The US Visual Artists Rights Act 1990 permits moral rights actions to the creators of listed works of visual art. It gives the creators:

- the right to claim authorship
- the right to prevent the use of one's name on any work the author did not create
- the right to prevent use of one's name on any work that has been distorted, mutilated or modified in a way that would be prejudicial to the author's honour or reputation
- the right to prevent distortion, mutilation or modification that would prejudice the author's honour or reputation
- and even the right to prevent the destruction of a work of art if it is of 'recognized stature'.

Performers' rights
Performers' rights are closely linked to copyright, but are not identical to it. This is the right of anyone who has conducted a public performance of some kind to authorize, or prevent a third party from recording, that performance. It explains why at music concerts, plays and so on there is often a ban on any recording of the performance. Performers also enjoy the moral right to be identified as a performer, and to object to any derogatory treatment of their performance. Under UK law, a performance is defined as a dramatic performance (including dance or mime), a musical performance, a reading or recitation of a literary work or 'a performance of a variety act or any similar presentation', whatever those last few words might mean. It appears that sporting events are not performances, though that is not 100% certain, when, for example, players in a team go through a practised routine. There is an arguable case that an extempore recitation or

any kind of lecture is a performance, even if it does include recitation from text. The performer can not only authorize or prevent recording of their performance, but also can authorize or prevent the making of copies of the recording, and the distribution of such copies to the public in any way, including electronic delivery. In UK law performers' rights currently (in 2012) last for 50 years from the end of the year of the original performance, but because of recently passed EU legislation, this will be extended to 70 years, probably in 2013 or 2014. At the moment there are no exceptions to performers' rights for, for example, non-commercial research or private study in the UK, but this may well change in the future.

WEB 2.0 POINT

Most of the performances that one is likely to encounter in Web 2.0 involve reproduction of music, films and the like within mashups or as part of a social networking site, such as YouTube or Facebook. Performers are often represented by organizations they have granted exclusive licences to, for example, within an exclusive recording contract. Many large music- and film-producing companies are aggressive (and understandably so) about protecting their performers' rights, and so anyone running a Web 2.0 service needs to think carefully about adopting a robust and effective notice and takedown procedure for dealing promptly with any complaints of infringement of performers' rights they receive; adopting a policy of moderating content uploaded by distributors to assess possible infringement of performers' rights (as well as other infringing material, of course); and getting undertakings from those who contribute that nothing they contribute infringe any IPR, including performers' rights.

Anyone submitting materials to a Web 2.0 service will probably be granting the service a licence to reproduce what is submitted. If what is being submitted includes performances, the submitter should ensure that performers' rights have been cleared with the performers, and should ensure that any licence they have signed up to when submitting materials protects their own performers' rights if it includes one of their own performances.

Trademarks

A trademark is a distinctive symbol that identifies through established use particular products or services of a trader to the general public. The symbol may consist of an image, words, or a combination of these. It can also be a particular colour, smell or shape under some circumstances. The owner in general enjoys the exclusive right to use the trademark in connection with the goods or services with which it is associated. Any person or firm that has a trade connection with the goods or services can obtain a trademark. The right may be lost if the trademark is not used, or indeed is so heavily used by others that it becomes a generic term (for example, Bayer lost the mark 'aspirin' when it became generic). The owner of a trademark may assign it or license others to use it. If, however, anyone uses a trademark 'in the course of trade' without the owner's permission, or uses a mark that is likely to be confused with a pre-existing trademark, the owner of the pre-existing mark can sue.

There are two types of trademarks: registered trademarks (RTMs) and unregistered trademarks, often known as trade names. An RTM, as its name implies, involves the formal registration of the mark, in the UK through the UK Intellectual Property Office or the European Trademark Office. There are forms to fill out and fees to be paid.

The protection only relates to the classes of product or service that the applicant registered the name for. Thus, 'food and drink' may be one class, 'dry cleaning services' another. It is therefore common that in a given country there are several identical registered trademarks, all perfectly valid, but each applying to a particular class of goods or services (to give an example, 'Apple' computers and 'Apple' records).

The owner has to pay renewal fees from time to time to keep the registered trademark in force, and must keep *using* the mark to keep it in force. The regulators rarely approve the granting of monopoly rights for areas of business in which the applicant is not currently active. There are certain defences against an infringement action, but they are limited in scope. Damages can be high. For this reason, there are risks if anyone copies logos and so on and puts them into a Web 2.0 application.

WEB 2.0 POINT

Any user of Web 2.0 services needs to ensure that they do not use without permission any third party trade names or RTMs as part of their service name, especially if those names or marks also relate to electronic services or software. Similarly, those who run Web 2.0 services should try to ensure that anyone contributing material to their service does not infringe any third party trademark rights, for example, by moderating all postings, or getting the contributors to confirm that nothing they submit infringes any third party IPRs. It is not difficult to carry out searches for particular registered trademarks in one's country of operation, though much harder to search for trade names. One obvious way of checking is to run the words (if they are words) through Google to see what comes up. In this way the owner of a Web 2.0 service can ensure that any name they give the service is not confusingly similar or identical to a RTM of an IT service of any kind.

Case study C

There have been cases where someone running a Web 2.0 service was threatened with trademark infringement by a foreign organization that happened to run an internet-based service in its country with the same name. In such cases, one should check if the organization doing the threatening is active in one's own country – a Google search should do the trick – as well as checking if the name has been registered in one's country. If the answer to both is 'no', then a robust reply is justified. If, however, the name (or one confusingly similar) *is* being used in countries where the Web 2.0 service is actively used, there is little choice but to change the name of the Web 2.0 service. However, dates are important; if the Web 2.0 service predates that of the complainant, the Web 2.0 service is entitled to insist the other service changes its name. For this reason, it is important to apply for a RTM as soon as possible and, in any case, to keep documented records of when the name was first used.

Case study D

In November 2011, BBC News reported that the German drug maker Merck KGaA had begun legal action against Facebook after discovering what its lawyer described as the 'the apparent takeover of its Facebook page'. The web page was being used by the German firm's US rival Merck & Co. A representative from Merck KGaA said that the social network 'is an important marketing device [and] the page is of great value', adding that since its competitor was benefiting from the move 'time is of the essence'.

A Facebook spokeswoman said: 'We are looking into it.' Merck KGaA said it had entered into an agreement with Facebook for the exclusive rights to www.facebook.com/merck in March 2010. The German firm said a number of its employees had been subsequently assigned administrative rights to the page. However, Merck KGaA said that when it had checked the site on 11 October 2010 it had discovered it had lost control of the page, and that content on the site now belonged to Merck & Co.

This case raises a couple of issues. It is clearly about the ownership of the rights to the URL, but it is odd that the German company Merck (which is completely separate from the American company with the superficially identical name) so rarely checked, let alone updated, the contents of its Facebook site. It is also unclear whether this is, in fact, a domain name dispute, a breach of contract by Facebook dispute, or both. Either way, the case both demonstrates the potential importance of the use of Facebook for marketing purposes, and the need to keep vigilant in checking that one's social networking sites never gets hijacked by a third party.

Domain names

Domain names and trademarks cover a lot of common ground, so both sections of this chapter should be read in conjunction with one another. The ground rules for domain names are well known; the first characters after the ubiquitous *www* are typically the full or shorthand name for the organization; the next characters (for example, *ac, org, com* or *edu*) give you a clue of the type of organization in question; and the final characters (*uk*) gives you the geographic location of the organization. The lack of any such geographic marker typically means the organization is in the USA.

Trademarks, whether registered or unregistered, are infringed if a third party uses the trademark for the same class of goods or services in a country where protection exists for it. It is not uncommon for different companies, which by coincidence are *in the same business*, to use similar or identical trademarks in different countries. In registered trademark and unregistered trade name law, this is not a problem, for in any one country, one of the marks will be the dominant mark, and other one simply cannot be used. But a quite different problem arises when we come to domain names. By definition, anyone anywhere in the world can create very similar domain names. So if two very similar domain names are created, can one of the owners sue the other for passing off (the term for an infringement action relating to unregistered trade names) or for infringement of registered trademarks?

Domain name disputes and legal problems can be broadly classified into a number of activities:

- two or more *bona fide* organizations legitimately claiming, owning or using the same or similar name or brand
- people opportunistically acquiring a valuable name, knowing a well known large corporation would want it; they may well then demand large sums of money (so-called cybersquatting) from the company to assign the domain name to them
- unofficial fan clubs wishing to adopt the name of their hero, team and so on, which may inconvenience officially sanctioned fan sites
- disgruntled people choosing to use variations of well known domain names to spread negative publicity about an organization
- misleading domain names; for example, the country code for Ascension Island is .ac, and that for Tuvalu is .tv; using domain names ending with those characters might lead a reader to believe that the URL is associated with a reputable academic institution, or a reputable TV company respectively
- using meta tags – indexing terms added to websites by the creator to ensure that the site is noted as a 'hit' when a search strategy is run on one of the

well known internet search engines; it does not necessarily appear in the title or the text of the web page.

There have been many cases decided over the years. The courts are agreed that the odd pieces (*www, com, org, uk* and so on) are irrelevant when considering a case; the key is the organization name and it is around that name that the dispute centres. This is because the characters before (for example, *www.*) and after (for example, *org.uk*) the organization's name are standard.

Consider the first type of dispute, with two organizations legitimately owning or using the same or similar name or brand in different countries. A good example is the *Prince plc v. Prince Sports Inc.* case, which was heard in both Britain and America in separate hearings. Typically, *the organization that first uses the domain name wins.*

What about the second type of case, where some people have claimed a valuable name knowing it would inconvenience a well known large corporation? They may well then demand large sums of money from the well known company to assign the domain name to them. Such cases have probably received the most publicity. Almost invariably, the organization demanding the money not merely loses the case (with costs to be paid), but also has the domain name in question forcibly taken from it and passed over to the larger company. Despite the clear-cut nature of the decisions so far, sooner or later someone is going to appeal and query the fundamental basis of the courts favouring the big boys against small entrepreneurs who have noted a market opportunity.

Case study E

In the late 1990s, Porsche was faced with an array of domain names free-riding on its name and reputation. These included: *porschecar.com, 928porsche.com, accessories4porsche.com, allporsche.com, beverlyhillsporsche.com, buyaporsche.com, myporsche.com, newporsche.com, parts4porsche.com, porsche-911.com, porsche-944.com, porsche-autos.com, porsche-carrera.com, porsche-cars.com, porsche-classic.com, porsche-sales.com, porsche-service.com, porsche4me.com, porsche4sale.com, porsche911.com, porsche911.net, porsche911.org, porsche911parts.com, porschecars.com, porschecarsales.com* and *porschedealer.com.*

These domain names had all been registered by different individuals or entities, many of who had given false information in the application procedure. Porsche requested the domain name registration certificates be transferred to Porsche, or forfeited, because they diluted their trademarks. However, the action, which was initiated in the USA, was dismissed. This demonstrates the problems large companies encountered in the past.

The third type of dispute, with unofficial fan clubs who wish to adopt the name of their hero, team and so on tend to be resolved by a threatening letter by the organization representing the team or individual. Courts in the next type of dispute, involving disgruntled people who have chosen to use well known names to spread negative publicity about a company, have normally found in favour of the companies. It is difficult to do much about misleading domain names other than making a complaint to the ISP hosting the site and asking it to take the site down.

The final type of dispute, on meta tags, depends on whether the courts consider the use of the particular tag was justified. If it were, the aggrieved party is unable to stop this apparent dilution of its mark.

The fundamental problem is that the internet is no respecter of national boundaries, and takes no account of the traditional way of carving up business activities that trademark owners are used to. The problem is exacerbated by the fact that there is no single central worldwide provider or assigner of such domain names that does a check before granting the name. Each country is largely responsible for its activities, and even in one country, an individual or organization may find competing services offering domain naming services.

WEB 2.0 POINT

Any domain names developed for one's service should not be identical to, or confusingly similar to, well established domain names in the same broad area of activity. Equally, once a domain name is established, one should check for anyone else setting themselves up with a similar or identical name. There are search services available that, for a fee, will check on the use of domain names, but one can do much for oneself by carrying out a Google search, or simply typing in some closely related domain names and seeing what comes up.

Case study F

(Adapted from www.bbc.co.uk/news/technology-15604222)
A Mr Marshall had registered the domain name waynerooney.co.uk in April 2002 after seeing the footballer play for Everton FC's youth team. However, he lost interest in the idea. Four years later, Wayne Rooney's company decided it wanted the web address. Its lawyers contacted Nominet, the organization that manages .uk domain names and requested the transfer. Mr Marshall was ordered to transfer the site because he had not shown any intention of using it after several years of ownership.

Mastercard tried to take ownership of maestro.co.uk for its debit card arm in 2006. The website was owned by Mark Adams, a domain name dealer who had also registered goldenarches.co.uk, bigbrothertv.co.uk and beverlyhillscop.co.uk among others. When contacted, Mr Adams said he 'would only consider selling it for an exceptional offer'. Surprisingly, Mastercard lost the case because Nominet ruled that 'maestro' was a generic name, and Mr Adams had done nothing to disrupt Mastercard's business. 'It is for the complainant to prove that the registration is abusive, not for the respondent to disprove it,' the adjudicator wrote. The decision was upheld on appeal.

Lockheed Martin set up Skunk Works in California in the 1940s. It became famous for developing aircraft including the U-2 spy plane and the F-117 stealth fighter. Just over 60 years later a small chain of shops called UK Skunkworks branched into internet sales with a web address using its name. The US firm demanded that Nominet transfer the domain name. Lockheed Martin claimed internet users were 'highly likely to mistakenly assume' the web address was associated with its operations and argued they might take their business elsewhere after seeing UK Skunkworks' goods. But the store owners issued a tongue-in-cheek defence retort: 'We do not sell or offer military services, stealth bombers, yo-yos, [or] decorations for Christmas trees.' The expert assigned to the case agreed there was little chance of confusion, and ruled against a transfer. Lockheed Martin appealed and lost again.

In 1992 a couple with the surnames Starker and Bucknell began a family newsletter dubbed the 'StarBuck Times'. When their brother-in-law subsequently registered the starbucks.co.uk domain name, he set up a clash with the world's biggest coffee chain. The firm became aware of the site in 1999 shortly after starting to trade in the UK. It was dismayed to find the web pages carried negative stories about its business and the company lodged a complaint with Nominet. Nominet's expert gave Starbucks ownership of the domain name.

Finally, consider the ihateryanair.co.uk website. The site gathered negative stories and complaints about the budget airline. Nominet ruled that the company's trademark had been used, even though there was little chance anyone would have believed the Irish company had been running the site. Ryanair now had to prove the site was disruptive to its business, and that the disruption was 'unfair'.

The site's owner had added adverts including links to a travel insurance firm and a foreign exchange provider. The airline offered rival services. Nominet ruled this 'unfair' on the basis that the Ryanair name had been used to attract traffic to the site, and so the site had to close down.

Patents

A patent is a bargain between an inventor (who may be an individual or an organization), and the state (or an official patent-issuing authority authorized by one or more states). In return for receipt of a full, clear description of the invention, the state grants the inventor a limited life monopoly on that invention. That monopoly means that no one may make, use, sell or import the invention without the patent-holder's permission during the period that the patent is in force. As with other types of IPR, the owner of a patent can sell (assign) it, or license others to use the invention (typically for a fee), while retaining ownership of the patent. The state, in turn, charges fees to the owner, both for the application for the patent and for its regular renewal, and also publishes the details of the invention (a so-called patent specification). Patent specifications can be obtained for a fee from patent-issuing authorities or some commercial providers, or, increasingly, users can obtain copies for free from various official and unofficial internet-based patent-information services.

There are certain key differences between patents and copyright. First, as already noted, the applicant for a patent has to go through an application process that involves paying fees and having the description of the invention subjected to tests to ensure it is valid. Second, again as already noted, the owner must pay regular fees to keep the patent in force. Third, the lifetime of a patent is much shorter than for copyright, being normally 20 years from the date when the invention was first the subject of a patent application anywhere in the world. Fourth, unlike copyright, where protection is automatic worldwide, for patents one has to apply for a patent in separate countries one wants protection in, with each application costing more money. On the other hand, patents give much stronger protection to the owner than copyright does. In the case of copyright, if I take a photograph of the Houses of Parliament, I own the copyright to my photo, but I cannot stop a third party taking a similar or identical photo at the same time using their camera, and reproducing their photo as they see fit. But if I acquire a patent to, say, a new chemical that has pharmaceutical properties, I can prevent another inventor who genuinely has made the same chemical, but applies for a patent one day after me, from both getting the patent and from making, using, importing or selling the invention for the time I keep the patent in force. Thus, the first person to file for a patent anywhere in the world for a major invention wins hands down over all their competitors.

In order to be granted a patent, the inventor must demonstrate that the invention passes the major (and pretty uniform) criteria set by patent offices around the world – i.e. must demonstrate that the invention is patentable. These are the main criteria:

- The invention has not been described to the public before the application date for the patent. Such a description might be in the form of a publication in any medium anywhere in the world (prior publication) or might be in the form of usage of the invention somewhere public before the date the patent was first applied for (so-called prior use).

- The invention must not be obvious to someone 'skilled in the art' – a notional expert in the field. This criterion has to be satisfied even if there has been no prior publication or prior use.
- The invention must be capable of 'industrial application' – in practice, this is not a major hurdle, and most inventions pass that criterion without difficulty.
- The invention must not be one of a list of things deemed unpatentable in law. Some of these are fairly obvious (for example, mathematical techniques), but some are not (for example, inventions contrary to public morality – which might include genetically engineered organisms – discoveries found in nature, surgical techniques, methods of playing games, literary works or computer programs). It is, incidentally, worth noting that despite the notional ban on computer programs, in practice, many computer programs do become the subject of patents where their action is tied to some 'industrial application'. The USA in particular is famous (or notorious) for allowing large numbers of often dubious computer program patents. The UK has taken a more restrictive approach, but even so many software patents exist in the UK as well.

WEB 2.0 POINT

It is unlikely that anyone other than software developers will encounter patents in connection with Web 2.0. However, software developers and those promoting Web 2.0 services need to be aware of the generosity of the US Patent and Trademark Office in granting software patents. If a Web 2.0 service is made available to US users, and it happens to use software that infringes a US patent, the service owners could find themselves at the receiving end of a patent infringement action. With the increasing pressure by the software industry to obtain a relaxation of the rules on software patents in the UK, it is possible that they might encounter such problems in the UK as well. On the other hand, some software developers might welcome a more relaxed stance by the UK Intellectual Property Office or the European Patent Office towards software patents, as it provides a second method of protection (as well as copyright, which is automatic and free of charge) for their software.

Answers to exercises
Exercise 1
In principle, all of these are capable of being considered databases. In the case of a personal library, much would depend on whether the items were arranged

in some systematic or methodical manner – something that would have to be considered subjectively. The e-mail thread is presumably in date order, which is arguably a systematic method of organization. Similarly, as long as the list of compounds was in some systematic order (alphabetical, by chemical formula and so on), the list will be a database. Note that it makes no difference whether or not the individual components enjoy copyright. Even if they do not, because they are out of copyright (First World War poetry) or because they are simple facts (bank statement elements, melting points and so on), the compilation is potentially a database. A single document can never be a database, but the document is almost certainly a single copyright work with multiple authors.

Exercise 2

The personal library might enjoy copyright as a literary work because the arrangement may well have involved intellectual effort. The resources expended in obtaining and verifying the data are trivial, so database right is unlikely to apply. On the other hand, a university library catalogue probably *did* involve significant investment in verifying and presenting the results, so would enjoy database right. But if the catalogue itself involved no intellectual creativity in its contents, no copyright applies. It depends a lot on what added value is offered by the cataloguers, for example, identifying details of the author and the contents. The selection of First World War poetry almost certainly will enjoy copyright, as the creator has chosen some and ignored others, and may also enjoy database right if effort was involved in obtaining, verifying and presenting the poems. The e-mail listing probably does not enjoy copyright because there is little intellectual about the collection, but might enjoy database right if there has been effort in obtaining and verifying the details.

The e-mail thread is unlikely to enjoy any protection. The bank statement is unlikely to be copyright as there is nothing original in the way the contents have been chosen or presented. Equally, its chances of enjoying database right are low. Depending on how and why the list of inorganic compounds were chosen, the list of melting points may enjoy copyright, and probably enjoys database right if there was effort in obtaining, verifying and presenting the contents. Although individual postings to Facebook may well enjoy copyright, because of the lack of intellectual effort involved, the entire collection would not. It is also unlikely that a list of Facebook postings would enjoy database rights.

Exercise 3

1. Because there are no moral rights associated with journal articles, no moral rights have been infringed. However, copyright probably has been infringed!
2. It really depends whether my critique is based on a fair selection of entries or not. There is also an arguable case that the folksonomy is a work of

reference, and therefore the creators do not enjoy moral rights anyway. In any case, it may be difficult to identify who has been subjected to derogatory treatment if this is genuinely a joint effort from several contributors.

3. This may be derogatory treatment, and it may also be copyright infringement of the words and/or music in the work. Whether it breaches the attribution right depends a lot on the age of the work; moral rights in performances do not apply to performances made before February 2006.

4. This is *prima facie* infringement of the right to object to something being attributed to Professor Peabody that they did not create.

CHAPTER 4

Data protection and privacy

Introduction

Most developed countries have at least a minimum level of data protection legislation in place; the USA is notable in having only limited protection at a federal level, although many states have introduced such legislation. On the one hand, everyone should have the right to freedom of expression, the freedom to hold opinions and to impart information and ideas without justified interference. On the other hand, every individual has the right to privacy – to be left alone. These two worthy concepts can, and do, sometimes collide.

Typically, a data protection law requires the following:

- Data controllers (those who manipulate data about individuals) must register with a supervisory body if they currently, or plan to, use personal data, and if that data can be searched or manipulated using the individual's name (or some code equivalent) as the search key.
- Data subjects (the individuals who have data about them stored and manipulated by third parties – every one of us) have the right to inspect what information is held about them.
- Data subjects have the right to demand to know whether data is held about them.
- Data subjects can sue for damage caused by inaccurate data about them, or for other breaches, such as unauthorized release of such data.
- Data controllers must abide by certain general principles and codes of practice.
- No doubt there would be exemptions for matters of national security, crime prevention and so on.
- There must be systems in place to prevent unauthorized access, deletion or amendment of records containing personal data.

However, some countries' legislation goes much further, for example, stating that:

- data controllers must explicitly request the permission of data subjects before handling their personal data
- data subjects can insist that data about them is deleted
- data subjects are entitled to know to whom data about them has been passed, and where data about them has come from
- no decisions about the data subject may be made purely relying on information obtained from personal data files.

UK data protection law

The UK's Data Protection Act 1998 (DPA) is an EU directive that has been transposed into national law. Thus, the data protection laws of all EU member states are very similar. The law is controlled by eight data protection principles, which are enumerated below:

1. Personal data shall be processed fairly and lawfully and, in particular, shall not be processed unless-
    a) at least one of the conditions in Schedule 2 is met, and
    b) in the case of sensitive personal data, at least one of the conditions in Schedule 3 is also met.

How does that translate into English? Without going into the details of the schedules referred to, it says that information must be obtained fairly, and even once obtained, it cannot be further processed (for example, stored, manipulated, disseminated, amended, destroyed and so on) unless certain conditions are fulfilled.

The data controller (the individual or organization responsible for collecting and manipulating the personal information) must inform each individual at the time of obtaining any personal information either directly, or when obtaining it from a third party, that it is collecting such information, unless this would involve what is called 'disproportionate effort'. Only a court case will decide what this term means but it really needs to be disproportionate. The method of informing the data subjects does not have to be an individual communication. For example, a general notice at the entrance to a car park that the premises are subject to CCTV recording is enough to inform anyone entering that car park.

Having collected the information legitimately, under what circumstances can the controller manipulate it in any way? Only if:

- the data subject (the individual concerned) consented to the processing, or the processing is for various contractual or legal and statutory purposes, or
- if processing is necessary: 'for the purposes of legitimate interests pursued by the data controller or by the third party or parties to whom the data are

disclosed, except where the processing is unwarranted in any particular case by reason of prejudice to the rights and freedoms or legitimate interests of the data subject'.

One or the other is certain to apply to the vast bulk of data processing going on in an organization, and so this part of the principle is easy to achieve.

'Processing' includes obtaining, recording, holding, disclosing and even disposing of information or data as well as carrying out any operation, or set of operations on it.

2. Personal data shall be obtained only for one or more specified and lawful purposes, and shall not be further processed in any manner incompatible with that purpose or those purposes.

An organization *must* identify in advance the purpose or purposes for which the data has been collected. This imposes a discipline on managers to be clear about what they are collecting data for.

3. Personal data shall be adequate, relevant and not excessive in relation to the purpose or purposes for which they are processed.

Accurate, but incomplete information is not legal. On the other hand, data should be relevant to the purpose intended without being excessive.

For example, what is irrelevant and excessive for routine invoicing may be perfectly acceptable for customer profiling and market research. Keeping a uniform amount of information about people simply for administrative convenience should be avoided.

Case study A

An employer required all new employees (male and female) to declare their chest size on the form used for new employees. When challenged, the employer stated that it needed this information so it could keep the right stocks of overalls for those employees doing dirty blue-collar jobs such as cleaning. But most employees did not do such jobs. The employer was found guilty of a breach of this principle and had to develop a new form for new white-collar employees.

4. Personal data shall be accurate and, where necessary, kept up to date.

Note the words 'where necessary'. Thus, for example, an employer is obliged to keep up to date information about its current employees, but is not obliged to chase an ex-employee to ensure that the person hasn't changed his or her address or name since leaving employment.

5. Personal data processed for any purpose or purposes shall not be kept for longer than is necessary for that purpose or those purposes.

In some instances, the length of time involved may be quite long; it will depend on the data and its application. The data controller has to make a sensible judgement here.

Exercise 1

Police have collected evidence about a suspect in a criminal case, but the case is later dropped for lack of sufficient evidence. How long should the police keep the data for?

---

6. Personal data shall be processed in accordance with the rights of data subjects under this Act.

A range of rights is prescribed in the Act for individuals about whom data is processed. They are described below. Someone holding personal data is breaking the law if they refuse to co-operate if an individual tries to exercise his or her rights.

7. Appropriate technical and organizational measures shall be taken against unauthorized or unlawful processing of personal data and against accidental loss or destruction of, or damage to, personal data.

'Processing' includes operations from collecting and acquiring data all the way through to its disposal. A judgement on what is necessary and appropriate is required. In determining reasonable security measures, consideration needs to be given to the cost of security, all the risks involved, both man-made and natural, and the sensitivity and value of the data and the consequences of compromising its integrity. The principle specifies that appropriate technical and *organizational* measures shall be taken. Security, therefore, is not simply a technology-related matter but involves organizations developing appropriate codes of practice and training staff to be aware of data protection. For example, the Act states: 'The data controller must take reasonable steps to ensure the reliability of any employees of his who have access to the personal data.'

8. Personal data shall not be transferred to a country or territory outside the European Economic Area unless that country or territory ensures an adequate

level of protection for the rights and freedoms of data subjects in relation to the processing of personal data.

The eighth principle prohibits the transfer of personal data to countries outside the EEA (the European Economic Area – the EU plus a couple of other European countries) that do not have 'an adequate level of protection'. Two questions follow: what is 'transfer', and what constitutes 'an adequate level of protection'?

'Transfer' includes the sending of the data abroad, whether in the form of paper, floppy disks, material on the hard disc of a portable computer, or by online means, to a country outside the EEA. Placing material on a website and allowing people in other countries to access and download it was the subject of a European court case, which decided it was not transfer. So 'transfer' means deliberate exporting of the data. It makes no difference whether the transfer is to third parties outside your own organization, or to people abroad within the organization. Therefore, executives carrying laptops and travelling from the UK to outside the EEA are just as problematic as the more obvious transfers.

The USA at present has no federal data protection law. So, transfer to the USA is *prima facie* illegal. However, there are some circumstances where such transfers are legal; they may only take place if one or more of the following apply:

- the individual gives consent to the transfer (this consent would be on a case-by-case basis; a vague blanket agreement is unlikely to be accepted by a court)
- where the transfer is necessary for the performance of a contract between the data subject and the controller
- where the data subject has requested the transfer as part of some pre-contractual arrangement
- where the data transfer is to fulfil a contract that is in the interests of the data subject
- where the transfer is necessary for important public interest grounds or for the fulfilment of legal claims
- where the transfer is to protect the vital interests (normally taken to mean health-related) of the data subject
- where the transfer is from a public register, which is there to provide information to the public.

Transfers to non-approved countries are also OK if they are made on (contractual) terms that are 'of a kind approved by the Commissioner'. Such a contract has to require that the recipient assumed UK data protection laws applied in their country. Good examples are so-called 'safe harbours' in non-EEA countries. These are organizations that commit to a set of privacy principles. Any data transferred is stored in the safe harbour and may not be transferred anywhere else (unless that, too, is a safe harbour). These may – and I stress 'may' – be acceptable to the Information Commissioner (see below). There are issues associated with safe harbours which are discussed in Chapter 7 on cloud computing.

Case study B

In November 2011, the Irish data protection authorities announced they would be carrying out an audit of Facebook's Irish offices following a complaint from a Facebook user. The complainant requested a copy of his personal data held by Facebook (see section 'The rights of data subjects' below). On receipt, he discovered that he had previously deleted much of the data that was included and consequently launched a media campaign, 'Europe v. Facebook', aimed at forcing Facebook to abide by European data protection laws. He has also filed 22 individual complaints with the Irish data protection authority, known as the Data Protection Commission (or DPC), which has jurisdiction over Facebook outside the USA and Canada, as the location of the Facebook international headquarters is Dublin.

Should the DPC discover that Facebook has indeed breached Irish data protection law, it may serve the social networking site with an order demanding it changes the way it holds personal data to ensure future compliance with data protection law.

Some definitions

'Data' is information that:

- is being processed by means of equipment operating automatically in response to instructions given for that purpose
- is recorded with the intention that it should be processed by means of such equipment
- is recorded as part of a *relevant filing system* or with the intention that it should form part of a *relevant filing system*
- forms part of an *accessible record*.

Information falling under any one of these headings constitutes 'data'. The first heading is computerized data; therefore, all computerized data containing personal information of any sort is subject to the Act. The term 'relevant filing system' is defined in the Act as:

> any set of information relating to individuals to the extent that, although the information is not processed by means of equipment operating automatically. . . the

set is structured, either by reference to individuals or by reference to criteria relating to individuals, in such a way that specific information relating to a particular individual is readily accessible.

Therefore, collections of papers in a folder that have no order or structure may be exempt from the 1998 Act. However, physical document collections with systematic ordering by a person's name or ID number are likely to fall within the remit of the Act. See Case Study C below.

The fourth heading ('accessible record') means certain health records created by a health professional, school records or a public record relevant to local authority housing or social services.

Only 'personal data' is subject to the Act. 'Personal data' is information relating to an identified, or identifiable, living individual. Data about corporations is not 'personal data'. An 'identified individual' is easy enough to understand. An 'identifiable individual' is someone who can be identified directly or indirectly from the information to hand. This could be by means of an ID number, by e-mail address, or some characteristic, associated with that individual. Thus the words 'the Prime Minister' refer to an identifiable individual, and a recognizable photograph of a person, even if he or she is not named, may well be personal data. The Act does not apply to data about dead people.

The individual is known as the *data subject*, who can be anybody in the world. As long as the data is under the control of a body that is UK-based, or is held in the UK, the Act applies.

Data can be in any medium, and so includes microfilm, movie film, CCTV video and so on, so long as information or images of living identifiable individuals that can be readily retrieved by a search on the person's name or ID, are involved.

Some personal data (sensitive personal data) is subject to even tighter control. This is data on:

- racial or ethnic origin
- political opinions
- religious or similar beliefs
- membership of trade unions
- physical or mental health
- sexual life
- commission, or alleged commission, of offences
- any proceedings for any offence committed or alleged to have been committed, the disposal of such proceedings and the sentence of any court in such proceedings.

Case study C

In October 2011, senior UK cabinet minister Oliver Letwin was caught disposing of letters sent to him from constituents into a waste bin in a park. In November 2011, confidential correspondence to another senior minister, Vince Cable, was found outside his constituency offices. Some of the letters related to constituents' medical history. On the face of it, this is sensitive personal data. However, the limitations of UK data protection law are highlighted because, although data in paper form is potentially covered by the Act, it has to be in a structured filing system before it is considered to be 'personal data'. Thus, a single letter, which has never been kept in a filing system, which is well structured, is exempt from the provisions of the Act.

In November 2011, Letwin received a mild slap on the wrist by the UK's Information Commissioner's Office (ICO), indicating that in the ICO's view, the data involved did qualify as personal data.

Note that – perhaps surprisingly – financial information is *not* considered to be sensitive personal information. Similarly, information about disciplinary proceedings against an individual, their exam or similar marks, or their DNA profile, is not sensitive personal data but just falls under the heading of personal data.

Such sensitive personal data can be processed, but only under strictly controlled circumstances. In contrast, 'ordinary' personal data is subject to more relaxed rules: the eight data protection principles.

Sensitive personal data in the public domain that has been made public as a result of steps deliberately taken by the data subject may be processed. Sensitive data needed for legal proceedings, including prospective proceedings, for obtaining legal advice, to defend legal rights, for the administration of justice and for the exercise of statutory or government functions can be processed. Processing sensitive personal data for ethnic monitoring – to check that an organization is fulfilling its obligations under racial equality laws – is also permitted.

Sensitive personal data can also be processed if the data controller obtains explicit written consent from the data subject. There is an implication that the consequences of any consent have been fully explained to the data subject.

The data controller is any individual or undertaking that determines the purposes for which, and the manner in which, personal data are or will be processed. It is perfectly possible to be a data controller without owning a computer; for example, the owner of files in a filing cabinet is a data controller. Also, the data may be held in another country, but the organization that gives instructions on its use is the data controller.

The Information Commissioner, who heads the ICO, oversees the administration of the Act and has certain legal duties under the Act. In addition to the Commissioner's duties, he or she has certain powers, which are important. These include:

- *Handling requests for assessment* – any person can ask the Commissioner for an assessment of whether processing of data is being carried out in compliance with the Act.
- *Serving information notices* – the Commissioner may serve an 'information notice' on any data controller demanding information within a specified time from the controller.
- *Serving enforcement notices* – the Commissioner may serve a notice requiring the data controller to amend, block, erase or destroy personal data.
- *Powers of entry* – the Commissioner has the right to ask a judge or sheriff for a warrant to enter and search premises.

The Commissioner also has various duties to disseminate information and guidance notes, and has the right to ask the Crown Prosecution Service to initiate legal actions and/or impose fines himself in cases of serious breaches of the Act.

The Act imposes two relatively simple obligations on data controllers: to notify the Commissioner of processing of personal data, and to abide by the data protection principles.

The rights of data subjects

In essence, data subjects have three rights:

- a right of access to inspect data held about them
- the right to prevent processing of data about them, including direct marketing data
- the right to sue for damage caused.

Any data subject, wherever he or she lives, has the right to be told if personal data is held about them on written request. He or she is also entitled to see, in a form that is understandable, *all* personal data held about them by the controller. There is a maximum fee that can be charged for this, but many organizations choose to make no charge for such requests.

The controller has 40 days to respond to the request once it has received the request in writing and any fee payable. The data must be provided in 'permanent form'. This usually means a paper copy, but *if* the data subject agrees, the data controller could pass the copy to him or her in the form of, say, a floppy disc containing the data.

If supplying any sort of information to the data subject is likely to identify another individual, the controller is entitled to delete that part of the data supplied unless the other individual has consented to this disclosure, or if it not reasonable to delete the data.

The data subject is entitled to make as many requests as he or she likes, as often as he or she likes, but a reasonable time must elapse between requests. Circumstances may arise where, when checking the data in response to a subject's request, it is found the data is inaccurate or misleading in some way.

There may be a temptation to correct the data before passing it to the subject. The law states that such data may not be amended before being supplied, nor may it be deleted, unless it was going to be amended or deleted routinely anyway.

The data subject is also entitled to know if the data controller is processing data about him or her so as to make an automated decision about the data subject. In such cases, the subject is entitled to a description of the decision-making process, but there is no obligation to supply this in a form capable of being understood by the data subject!

The data subject is also entitled to prevent any processing that is causing, or is likely to cause 'unwarranted and substantial damage or distress' to either themselves *or to others*. In the case of direct marketing, the data subject need not even claim damage or distress.

The data subject can ask a court to order correction, erasure or blocking of any data that is false or factually misleading.

The data subject is entitled to claim compensation for any breach of the Act that has resulted in damage. Where there is quantifiable financial damage, further damages for distress can be demanded. Where the data has been processed for use by the media, claims may be for distress alone.

Exemptions

The exemptions vary according to the particular circumstances and nature of information and its use. This section only mentions a few. There are many others, and if you are advising others in your organization, you need to check the exemptions carefully.

Journalism, literature, art

There are exemptions for publishing material containing personal information that falls in these special purposes. In this context, 'publishing' is defined as making data available to the public or any section of the public, and so potentially includes all types of postings to Web 2.0 services.

The following exemptions apply:

- all the data protection principles except the seventh (it therefore remains important to maintain appropriate security arrangements against, for example, theft, loss or computer hacking)

- data subject access rights
- the data subject's right to prevent processing likely to cause damage or distress
- the data subject's rights in relation to automated decision-taking
- the data subject's rights to data rectification, blocking, erasure and destruction.

The exemption is designed to enable freedom of expression and the conduct of activities such as investigative journalism in the public interest. The exemption is on a case-by-case basis, and should not be regarded as a blanket exemption. It only applies to personal data being processed *with a view to publication*. The exemptions even extend to sensitive personal data, and so an academic writing an article, say, about a politician's interesting sex life benefits from the exemption.

The exemption applies only to publication 'in the public interest', whatever that might mean. Finally, the data controller must reasonably believe that compliance with the relevant provision of the Act (for example, a data subject's request to see what is held about him or her) is incompatible with freedom of expression. In other words, giving the individual access would prevent in total or in part the publication of text that should be published in the public interest. The aggrieved individual is entitled to take the controller to court to get a judgment whether the exemption should apply or not.

Research, including history and statistics
Researchers that use personal information enjoy certain exemptions, as long as the information is not processed:

- to support measures or decisions with respect to particular individuals
- in such a way that substantial damage or substantial distress is, or is likely to be, caused to any data subject.

Information available to the public by or under enactment
Information is often made available to the public as a legal requirement under an act, for example, the Register of Electors. Such information is exempt from certain of the Act's provisions.

Confidential references given by a data controller
The *writer* of a reference is not obliged to provide the data subject with access to its contents. The *recipient* of the reference, however, IS obliged to show a data subject the references he or she has received unless such a disclosure would breach someone else's privacy, for example, the reference writer's, or someone else named in the reference.

WEB 2.0 POINT

All Web 2.0 uses have the potential to be subject to data protection legislation. Any information in electronic format that includes individuals' names, and which is searchable by an individual's name, is potentially subject to data protection legislation. The sorts of data that fall into this net include:

- references to a living, identifiable individual by name or by some other criterion (for example, a job title or ID number if unique to that person), for example, in the body of text or in the header
- an image of a person if that person is identifiable (for example, a tagged photograph on Facebook)
- the name of someone who has posted, or re-posted something.

Even in circumstances where the data is anonymized, users may be identified through their behaviour, and/or the piecing together of related data. The Web 2.0 application must register that it holds personal data, allow individuals the right to inspect records about themselves, correct any errors about individuals on the services, and have certain minimum standards to prevent unauthorized access to personal data, which reflects the value and sensitivity of information held. Most of the requirements are sensible and cover what any prudent or well run operator would expect; but some are not so straightforward: they may not realize, for example, that the requirement for accuracy means an individual can demand that an error in an item referring to them must be corrected or else the person or organization running the Web 2.0 application is breaking the law.

Transfer of data outside the EEA

It is a breach of the DPA to transfer personal data outside the EEA unless the country where the data has been transferred to has what are considered to be adequate data protection laws, or the person has consented to such a transfer, or where the transfer is into a so-called safe harbour (a physical area where the regulations are as strong as if it were subject to the DPA), or in a few other cases, for example, it is necessary for the implementation of a contract, or is legally required. 'Transfer' here means the deliberate sending of the data to the other country. It does not appear to include merely placing certain data on, say, a website so that someone in another country could draw it down.

A good example of where personal data is transferred outside the EEA with the person's consent is Facebook. You can control how your content is shared through privacy settings; the default settings may be set to disclose more information than you would like to. When you publish content using the 'Everyone' setting, it means that anyone will be able to access that content.

Controversially, Facebook can use any content you post on or in connection with Facebook. It appears that even if you later delete content, Facebook retains it. Facebook applications and platforms have their own agreements in place as to how they use the content you share. Because Facebook is based in the USA, which famously has no federal data protection law, if you submit personal data voluntarily to it, you cannot complain about how Facebook subsequently uses it.

WEB 2.0 POINT

A Web 2.0 service might transfer personal data to third parties that are contracted to provide a service. Such sharing of personal data requires compliance with the DPA. This can raise issues relating to seeking consent and when and how such consent should be sought. Note that any external service that provides hosting and software services for a Web 2.0 service is subject to the data protection laws (if any) of its home country. Therefore great caution should be applied before committing any personal data to be run by an organization based outside the EEA. This topic is explored more fully in Chapter 7 of this book.

Apart from the legal responsibilities it imposes on data controllers, those who contribute to Web 2.0 applications run risks of identity theft, financial loss, loss of business or employment opportunities and physical harm. An example is where a user becomes the victim of a stalker as a result of the availability of their online profile.

Case study D

There have been a number of cases of data protection breaches by users of Facebook. To give just three examples from 2011: a nurse was dismissed from Nottingham University Hospitals Trust after posting a picture of a patient on Facebook. The case was one of 29 reported breaches of patient confidentiality at the trust over the past three years. A total of eight members of staff were dismissed over the breaches. There is an arguable case that the Trust itself is in breach of the DPA for failing to ensure sufficient technical and organizational measures were in place to prevent such breaches.

In a separate case, a Lloyds Bank employee was dismissed for posting a picture on their Facebook page of 'a typical day at work' in which bank customer details were visible in the background. In the final case, a cleaner at a hospital was dismissed. He had noticed a female patient in Accident and Emergency whom he took a liking to, checked out her details on her case notes, and then contacted her using Facebook suggesting they meet. In this latter case, in November 2011, the hospital in question was also clearly at fault since, because of the lax way it processed such personal data, it had allowed an unauthorized individual to access personal details of patients. It will be interesting to see if the ICO takes up this particular case.

Cookies

In May 2011, UK law on cookies changed, though the changes only came into effect in May 2012. The changes implement revisions to the European Directive on which the UK legislation is based. Cookies and similar technologies can only be placed on a user's machine where the user has given their consent. Consent may be signified by a user who amends or sets controls on their internet browser or by using another application or programme to signify consent.

A cookie is a piece of text stored on a user's computer by their web browser. They have a range of uses, including authentication, storing site preferences and shopping basket contents. They are categorized according to their duration and who sets them. Some only last for the duration of the session, while others are stored on the user's computer and can be accessed repeatedly by the organization that set it up on first contact.

The new law requires that users must provide their consent before websites can download cookies (and their equivalents) onto the user's machine via the browser. All EU countries were required to implement this change into their national legislation by May 2011. Cookies that are necessary to provide a service that the user has asked for, for example, to fill a shopping trolley, are exempt from this legislation. However, the new legislation does cover situations where cookies are used for things the user has not requested, such as the delivery of ads. The new laws apply to all organizations that download cookies onto the machines of users based in the EU, *whether those organizations are based in the EU or not.*

In the UK, the Department for Innovation, Business and Skills has stated that it favours the approach of user consent to be given using browser settings, rather than requiring website owners to implement pop-up windows every time a cookie is to be used. Until the legislation and accompanying guidance is produced, there are still some practical steps any website owner – including Web 2.0 service owners – should do:

- Check that your privacy statement covers cookie usage. It should explain clearly what kind of information is being collected, and for what purpose. If you are using third party cookies explain what these companies are and why you are sharing data with them. Consider providing information or links to assist in cookie removal.
- Keep track of what cookies are being set by your site. Identify which ones are impacted by this legislation. The most common applications of third party cookies are for advertising, social media links and visitor activity trackers.

WEB 2.0 POINT

The controller of a Web 2.0 application needs to provide information about cookies and obtain consent before a cookie is set for the first time. Provided they get consent at that point, they probably do not need to do so again for the same person each time the same cookie is used for the same purpose.

The Web 2.0 service must gain consent by giving the users information about what they are agreeing to and providing them with a way to show their acceptance. The only exception is if the cookie is 'strictly necessary' for a service requested by the user. The exception would not apply, for example, just because it is more attractive if the service remembers users' preferences or if the service operator decides to use a cookie to collect statistical information about use of a website.

Exercise 2

A Web 2.0 service is available all over the world. Does the owner of the service, which is run from the UK, have to worry about the data protection implications of this?

Case study E

The operators of a social networking space established to research and study interactions between users of the site with a view to developing the optimum environment for learning want to keep records of the users of the site but they are unsure as to what constitutes personal data within the meaning of the DPA.

Personal data within the meaning of the DPA is data from which a living individual can be identified. Even if an individual is not immediately recognizable from a piece of datum, he or she may become identifiable by combining data in the possession of the data controller or which may come into the possession of the data controller. The key is whether the individual can be identified. Examples whether singly or collectively include pictures, e-mail addresses, telephone numbers and place of work.

Exercise 3

The operators of the social networking space also want to take photographs of the subjects using the site. Can they do this?

Exercise 4

The owners of the social networking site have asked a software consultancy to help them store and sort through the data collected on the site. They have heard the terms 'data controller' and 'data processor' but are unsure how they relate to their project and what obligations there might be under the act for the processor and controller of data.

Exercise 5
The data gathered by the owners of the social networking site includes information on the participants' religious beliefs. Are there any special provisions that need to be taken into account under the DPA?

New laws coming?
In November 2011, the EU Justice Commissioner Viviane Reding, Vice-President of the European Commission, and the German Federal Minister for Consumer Protection, Ilse Aigner, issued a joint statement claiming that proposals to reform the 1995 Data Protection Directive would be published by the end of January 2012. Although at the time this chapter was written full details were not available, based on the tenor of the announcements made so far, the proposals are likely to strengthen the rights of data subjects and restrict further the ability of data controllers to process personal data without explicit permission from the data subjects. Somewhat surprisingly, what is being recommended is an EU regulation rather than an EU directive; regulations are rarely used by the EU and give Member States no leeway in the way they are implemented. The proposed new regulation contains some interesting provisions, including: DNA profiles to be included as sensitive personal data; new obligations on data controllers to appoint data protection officers, and an obligation to give them the resources and authority to carry out their duties; an obligation of controllers to inform the supervisory body within 24 hours of any breach, and to inform data subjects within 24 hours if the breach endangers their personal data; an obligation on national governments to give their supervisory bodies sufficient monies to operate effectively; and the setting up of a European Data Protection Board to advise the Commission. The new directive is also likely to extend the coverage of data protection legislation to larger swathes of manual data, and to increase the punishments for breaches of data protection laws. However, one can expect a lot of lobbying on these topics, and it is unlikely that a regulation will get passed, let alone transposed into EU member states' laws, before 2015.

Answers to exercises
Exercise 1
It depends on the seriousness of the alleged offence, and is a particularly problematic judgement call for police forces. A scandal some years ago (the Soham murders case) showed that some police forces were routinely, and arguably incorrectly, deleting information about suspects very soon after deciding

not to pursue a case. But on the other hand, retaining such information indefinitely strikes a lot of people as unfair.

Exercise 2

The fact that the service is available worldwide is irrelevant from UK law point of view. The DPA applies if the data is held in the UK, or control of the data is held in the UK. Thus the service provider must abide by the DPA. It further depends whether the personal data is being actively exported abroad, or simply happens to be available to someone in another country. If the latter, then court decisions indicate that the Web 2.0 service controller has nothing to worry about. But it would be a matter of concern if, say, personal data was actively *sent* by the Web2.0 service to someone in the USA. In other words, 'push' services are problematic, but 'pull' services, where the recipient has to do something to retrieve the information, are not.

It is likely that if the service is available in other countries, it will be subject to the laws of those countries as well, for example, in regard to defamation, pornography, terrorism and so on, and it may well be that the laws in question are very different in those countries than in the UK. Local legal advice should therefore be sought to ensure the service, while running legally from the point of view of UK data protection law, does not infringe other countries' laws.

Exercise 3

For the DPA, whether the operators could process the photographs would depend on whether the data (the photograph) was personal data within the meaning of the DPA. Note also that by combining data the individual may well become identifiable, even if he or she was not identifiable from the photograph. A ruling of the European Court of Human Rights in January 2009 held that the taking of a photograph without consent – whether or not it is subsequently published – is a violation of the right to privacy guaranteed by Article 8 of the European Convention on Human Rights. So in all cases permission should be sought to take photographs whether or not they will subsequently be published on the site.

Exercise 4

Under the DPA, the 'data controller' is the person 'who (either alone or jointly or in common with other persons) determines the purposes for which, and the manner in which, any personal data are, or are to be, processed'. In contrast, a 'data processor' is a person who processes the data on behalf of the data controller. The Act places the legal obligations regarding processing (that it be in accordance with the data protection principles) on the data controller. So it would be essential for the owners of the site (or their employers) to have a contract with the software consultancy (the data processor) detailing the manner in which the processing should be carried out.

Exercise 5

The DPA classes information about an individual's religious beliefs as sensitive personal data. If sensitive personal data is to be processed, additional obligations are placed on the data controller. The subject needs to give explicit consent to the processing of the information, meaning that some kind of affirmative action is required, such as written consent or clicking on an 'I agree' button on a web page.

CHAPTER 5

Freedom of information

Introduction

Freedom of information (FoI) is legislation that obliges government and other public bodies to reveal information (often in the form of internal documents) to the public. Many countries around the world, including England and Wales, Scotland (which has similar but distinct legislation) and the USA, have adopted FoI legislation. The Act controlling the law in England and Wales is the Freedom of Information Act 2000. The Freedom of Information (Scotland) Act 2002 governs Scots law. At the time this book was written, there was no FoI legislation covering Northern Ireland. Unlike the DPA, the UK's FoI laws are not tied to any EU directive. There is separate, and even stronger legislation covering information of relevance to the environment (the Environmental Information Regulations 2004, and similar Scots legislation), but that is not considered further in this chapter.

A basic purpose of FoI legislation is to reduce the public's distrust of government. It improves democracy by giving the public greater access to the workings of government, and a better-informed electorate presumably ensures better government. It reduces the need for whistle-blowing and leaks, and reduces the chances that governments and government-related bodies make expensive mistakes or corrupt decisions. In the UK, FoI legislation was only passed with great reluctance by the then Labour Government, and Tony Blair, the then prime minister, is on record as saying that the legislation was the worst mistake he made when prime minister – a remark that would be viewed with surprise by many. Even having been passed, the England and Wales Act has very wide exemptions, which make it less than useful for many purposes. Thus, for example, it was only after many struggles over the applicability of the Act that Heather Brooke, the campaigner, finally uncovered the scandal of parliamentary expenses. This case set a precedent that the UK Government cannot refuse to disclose details about a public sector employee's salary band and/or expenses.

There is a degree of tension between any FoI act and data protection legislation, as the latter is designed to prevent the unauthorized disclosure of information about individuals, while the former tries to expose as much information as possible. Thus, for example, while arguably information about the health of the prime minister is of value to the public when assessing the actions of his or her government, such revelations would clearly be a breach of the DPA. FoI legislation resolves this by ensuring that data protection always trumps FoI if there is a conflict and if disclosure would be 'unwarranted'. Of course, that leaves open to debate what is, or is not, unwarranted.

Incidentally, there is separate legislation that requires many government bodies to hand over (for a fee, which reflects the cost of reproduction only) commercially valuable data or information to anyone who requires it for their own purposes, including commercial purposes. The idea behind this is to encourage entrepreneurs to make use of valuable information if they can, as a result, generate income from it and thereby improve economic conditions. The entrepreneur does not have to be UK based. Thus, for example, census data that is available could be copied and used by a service offering genealogical research. FoI legislation, incidentally, is unrelated to the public's access to old records at the Public Record Office – that is covered by the Public Records Act 1958.

Some details

The law in the UK gives any person the right to know if a public authority holds certain information, and to obtain copies of said information. The person making the request can be anyone anywhere in the world. No questions should be asked about their motives for asking. The requestor can use a pseudonym if required, but if he or she does, then they have no right of appeal against a refusal to supply the information. The Act has an associated code of practice. While there is no legal obligation to follow this code, in practice most bodies do.

The Act refers to 'information', and defines this term as 'information recorded in any form'. This is not as silly a definition as one might first think, because of the key word 'recorded'. This means the information must be recorded, for example, in print, handwriting, audio, video, or of course in any digital form. The information in question may form part or all of a single document, or might be scattered among many recorded items. If the information happens to include references to a living identifiable person and disclosure might breach the DPA, the responding public body is entitled to edit the document to remove such personal details before handing a copy or summary of it over. If on the other hand the document is solely about an individual, then, as noted above, there may be grounds simply to refuse the requestor permission to view the item.

The information has, of course, to be held by a public authority, or by someone on behalf the public authority. It does not have to be physically in the UK, as long as the authority is based in the UK. Information that has been routinely deleted, or was about to be routinely deleted, can be ignored when responding to an FoI request. In principle, the law is very tough on anyone who chooses to delete information rather than disclose it as a result of receiving a FoI request, but in practice it can be very difficult to prove that such a deletion occurred, or was as a result of a FoI request. If the material was held in electronic format, backup files need to be checked as well as the current one. Of course, if the public authority genuinely never held the information, it is entitled to say that to the requestor. In other words, it is not obliged to start collecting certain information just because a requestor has asked for it.

There is a long (and growing from time to time) list of organizations under the Act deemed to be public authorities. They include government departments, Parliament, the armed forces, local government bodies, fire authorities, the NHS, schools, colleges, universities, the British Council, police forces, HM Revenue & Customs, etc. In some cases, the BBC, Channel 4 and some other bodies are subject to the Act, as are nationalized organizations and the Press Complaints Commission. However, banks that were (at the time of writing) majority owned by the Government, such as Royal Bank of Scotland, are not subject to FoI legislation. Certain private companies that perform public services, such as Group 4 (prisons and detention centres) and refuse collection companies are also subject to FoI. Water, gas and electricity companies are subject to environmental information regulations, but not FoI. Some bodies, such as the Secret Service and other intelligence services are not subject to the Act, and much information held by the police, for example, on anti-terrorism measures, will be refused; the grounds for refusal are considered below.

Exercise 1

An investigative journalist wishes to know how much money is spent by a public authority on staff parties. How should the authority respond?

In addition to the obligation to supply information, all public authorities are obliged to develop and publish (typically on the web) a 'publication scheme'. These link to documents proactively made available to the public by the organization. One side effect is the need for a member of staff to create and maintain such publication schemes; often these are library and information professionals.

All requests for FoI information must be made in writing (which can include e-mail, and probably also text messages and Twitter messages) to the public authority. There is no obligation to respond to oral requests, for example by phone, though many bodies do so. The requestor must give a name or pseudonym and contact address – which could be an e-mail address. A full description of the required information should be provided. There is no obligation to use the phrase 'freedom of information', and so staff need to be trained to recognize that any request for information might fall under the legislation and therefore must be complied with. The public authority is obliged to assist if the requestor has difficulty expressing their request – or should recommend where the requestor should go to help formulate their request properly. It is not clear what obligations rest on the public authority if the request is made in a foreign language.

The public authority is entitled to charge a fee to cover its costs in collecting the information, and while many do, some do not bother to. The information must be supplied within a maximum of 20 days from receipt of the request, or the fee, whichever is the later. In some exceptional circumstances the length of time can be extended. Failure to fulfil a request within the time limit can lead to problems if the requestor makes a complaint to the Information Commissioner. The maximum fee for long and complex requests can be high, or, if the amount of work required is considered excessive, the authority can decline to fulfil the request. However, in such cases, the authority is obliged to inform the requestor and advise on how to make the request more manageable. Photocopying costs can be added to the fee where appropriate. Proposed fees can be challenged by the requestor by going to the Information Commissioner to make a complaint. The authority must provide the information requested in a form that suits the requestor. It must be a permanent copy, for example, on paper, on a memory stick and so on as the requestor prefers. Alternatively, the applicant can be invited to the authority's premises to inspect the material. Full text documents or a summary can be offered. The final decision on these options is normally the requestor's, not the authority's. The authority can refuse a request it considers vexatious (for example, from someone who simply wants to cause problems to the authority by asking for large amounts of information every few days) or excessive.

It is an offence deliberately to hide or delete information held by the public authority in response to a FoI query, but there may be a problem in proving that intentional deletion occurred.

It should be noted that in addition to the tension between FoI and data protection, there is a tension between FoI and copyright. Although the requestor is entitled to receive the information requested in permanent form, that does not necessarily give him or her the right to reproduce it further. This is because the materials offered to the requestor are the subject of copyright, belonging either to the public authority or some third party. However, and here is a real curiosity in UK law, an Information Commissioner's decision declared that it is *not* unlawful to place the materials received onto a website. It is difficult to give clear advice on what can, or cannot, be done with materials received as a result of an FoI request, as a court may in future decide either that everything obtained via FoI can be copied, or nothing can be. But right now, it seems one cannot photocopy or print it out, but one can put it on the web. It should also be noted that the information may not be in the form of a document, but might be a collection of data, which may or may not be protected by copyright and/or database right.

FoI and research

There are also issues relating to research – see Case Study A below.

Case study A

University of Essex carries out intensive research on the evidence for global warming, a controversial subject in some commentators' eyes. Some critics of global warming attempted to obtain details of data collected by the University using FoI legislation. The University originally refused, but was later required to disclose the data by the Information Commissioner. The resulting publicity gave the impression that the University was trying to hide data that ran contrary to the consensus that global warming is happening and is due to increasing carbon dioxide levels.

Perhaps as a result of this, the ICO has issued advice on the handling of requests for information about research being undertaken by public bodies – see www.ico.gov.uk/news/latest_news/2011/ico-issues-advice-on-the-disclosure-of-research-information-26092011.aspx. What this says, in fact, applies to all types of FoI requests:

- *The public interest test* – The guidance highlights the importance of the public interest test and factors in favour of disclosure that should be considered.
- *Commercial information* – Many public bodies work in partnership with third parties and hold commercially sensitive information relating to those partners. If there is a genuine need to protect information from disclosure, it can be refused.
- *Free and frank discussion* – The guidance acknowledges the importance of academics and researchers being able to exchange views internally and to formulate and debate opinions relating to research away from external scrutiny. Protection for this type of information is provided by section 36 of the Act (prejudice to the conduct of public affairs).
- *Vexatious requests* – While most requesters use the legislation responsibly, there is occasionally some misuse of the rights provided by the law – or circumstances where requests become overly burdensome, disrupt a public authority's ability to perform their core functions, or appear to be part of an intention to disrupt or attack the public authority's performance. The guidance highlights the provisions under the law, which give some exceptions to the duty to deal with such requests.

- *Proactive disclosure* – The guidance emphasizes the benefits of proactive disclosure of information, acknowledging the public interest in their work.
- *Personal e-mail accounts* – The guidance confirms that if it is related to public authority business then such e-mails are subject to disclosure under the legislation. When searching for information in response to requests, staff should consider if it is appropriate to ask colleagues if information is held in a personal e-mail account. The ICO recommends that official work is stored on properly secure networks rather than personal e-mail accounts.

Exemptions

Arguably the most controversial area of the UK's FoI laws is the long list of exemptions to obligations under the law. There are two types of exemption – absolute (which require no explanation) and qualified (where the authority has to justify why it is refusing to supply the information). Absolute exemptions would be made in the following circumstances:

- The information is already available.
- The information relates to national security.
- The information relates to the administration of justice.
- The information would breach parliamentary privilege (but this failed in the case of MP expenses).
- This is personal information covered by data protection.
- This is information which, if revealed, would lead to an action for breach of confidence (marking something as 'confidential' is not enough to enjoy this exemption).
- Disclosure would be a breach of the law, for example, contempt of court, defamatory and so on.

Exercise 2

Someone puts in a FoI request to get the address of a refuge where people who have escaped abusive partners are sheltering. Should the public authority supply this information?

Even with absolute exemptions, the applicant is entitled to appeal to the Information Commissioner if they do not like the decision.

There is a long list of qualified exemptions, where the authority has to apply a public interest test: what is more important, keeping the information confidential or releasing it? The onus is on the public authority, but the applicant can appeal against a decision. Among these qualified exemptions are:

- information intended for future publication (it must be genuinely intended, not just vaguely planned)
- information relating to defence or security matters
- information relating to international relations, or relations between the government and the devolved administrations of Wales, Northern Ireland and Scotland
- criminal investigations and proceedings
- the auditing of public bodies
- formulation of government policy
- information relating to the country's economic performance
- information that could affect people's health and safety
- information that would prejudice the conduct of public affairs
- information relating to legal professional privilege
- trade secrets or any information that is likely to prejudice the commercial interests of any person or organization
- information relating to the royal family
- information relating to the honours system.

This is a much longer list of exemptions than in most other countries with FoI legislation, and some of these headings are so broad as to potentially defeat the whole object of FoI. Although the requestor can appeal to the Information Commissioner, his or her powers, as we shall see, are somewhat limited.

The Information Commissioner
In many countries with both FoI and data protection legislation there are two separate bodies responsible for overseeing the administration of the laws. In the UK, both sets of responsibility lie with the Information Commissioner's Office, better known as the ICO. The Information Commissioner can demand details of responses from public authorities and issue orders following an investigation after a complaint has been received from a requestor. He or she can also impose some penalties on authorities that break the law. As with data protection, he or she also has the right to inspect premises and, if need be, get a warrant to enter premises.

There is a tribunal (the Information Tribunal) which can hear appeals against the Information Commissioner's decision on anything to do with either FoI or data protection. However, and this is what seriously weakens the applicability of FoI legislation in the UK, in some circumstances the Government can veto a ruling relating to FoI from either the Commissioner or from the Tribunal, as, for example, it did in May 2012 regarding the risks relating to a controversial reorganization of the NHS. Thus, ultimately, the Commissioner cannot impose his or her will on a recalcitrant government. There are other problems with the Commissioner's role, too. He or she does not have enough staff to investigate all the data protection and FoI complaints the ICO receives, and this, combined with the wide exemptions granted under FoI legislation, makes the law far less robust than it might seem at first glance. There is also a wide range of information that is outwith the scope of FoI legislation, such as fire safety reports on premises.

WEB 2.0 POINT

It is possible that some public authorities maintain Web 2.0 services, or that some individuals who work for public authorities contribute to Web 2.0 sites. Furthermore, some Web 2.0 sites may well include materials obtained under FoI requests.

FoI law would require that a public authority that runs a Web 2.0 service should pass over any materials relevant to that service on request from any person unless such materials fall under one of the exemptions. Public authorities should also respond to FoI requests relating to their use of Web 2.0. However, as noted above relating to copyright, the legality of placing materials obtained by a FoI request onto a Web 2.0 server is unclear. It is therefore recommended that until the law is clarified on this matter that administrators should ensure that their Web 2.0 service does not include materials clearly obtained from an FoI request, and, as usual, should require a warranty from contributors that nothing they submit to the Web 2.0 service infringed copyright or database right.

It is an open question as to whether an FoI request made through a Web 2.0 medium, for example, on Facebook or on Twitter, is one the public authority is obliged to respond to. No doubt a court case sometime in the future will help clarify this.

Answers to exercises
Exercise 1
This is a perfectly valid request and the authority is obliged to respond.

Exercise 2
The authority would be justified in refusing this request because its disclosure could cause people physical or financial damage, so this qualifies as an absolute exemption under confidential information.

CHAPTER 6

Defamation

Introduction

This chapter reflects the law of defamation in early 2012. In May 2012 the Government introduced a Defamation Bill to revise the law of defamation – see www.publications.parliament.uk/pa/bills/cbill/2012-2013/0005/13005.i-i.html. Readers are urged to check the progress of this Bill, as it will probably have significant impact on defamation law in England and Wales. A person – an individual or an organization – can sue if someone writes or says something about them that causes them damage. Often, this is not just financial damage, but damage to reputation. In England and Wales, there are two types of defamation. Libel is a defamatory statement in fixed format, such as on paper, in an e-mail, in a tweet or Facebook posting or in a phone text message. Slander is when the defamatory statement is made orally, but has no permanence, for example, no audio recording was made of it. In the case of Web 2.0, it is in fixed format, and so like other internet-related cases (see below) would be considered to be libel. Incidentally, Scots law does not recognize the concept of slander.

There is a real danger of libel or slander on Web 2.0 services. The informal style of some of the messages encourages informal responses, as does the use of smileys such as :-), ;-) and :-(to indicate the sense in which a person is sending a message. For some obscure psychological reasons that are difficult to understand, when people send a message by keyboarding to screen and pressing the send button, they sometimes include comments that can be far stronger and more abusive than people would care to put on paper, or say to the third party. Maybe it is this lack of non-verbal clues, or the anonymity provided by the internet, that encourages such risky statement making. Even so it is astonishing that they do not realize the risks they are taking, but that is a fact of life.

To be considered defamatory, the statement must tend to be, or be, likely to lower the reputation of the defamed person among reasonable people who have read or heard the statement. Interestingly, one does not have to *prove* reputational damage, simply that in the minds of right-minded people this is likely to occur, though, of course, the more evidence that can be found that people really were influenced by the defamatory statement, the higher the damages are likely to be. All of this implies, of course, that the defamed person enjoys a good reputation; it would be difficult for, say, a convicted criminal, to argue the case that their good reputation had been damaged. Equally, one cannot defame a dead person.

Case study A

Robert Maxwell, the CEO of Maxwell Online, died in mysterious circumstances in November 1991 at a time when he was pursuing libel actions against both the BBC and *Private Eye*. His death meant that all these actions died with him. Following his death, revelations about the way he cheated his company of pension fund money emerged. It is safe for this book to report this, since Mr Maxwell is dead.

Typically, the legal action taken by the defamed person is to sue for damages. In a few cases in the past, criminal actions were instituted, though this is no longer possible. Normally, the case is heard before a jury, which, unusually, not only decides if defamation has occurred, but also decides the damages to be awarded if defamation is confirmed. Juries in the UK in years gone by famously awarded massive damages, reaching millions of pounds, but these days damages tend to be more modest. However, legal costs can add heavily to the losing party's woes, as they can reach hundreds of thousands of pounds in a major case. If both parties agree, the case can be heard in front of a single judge, who decides if defamation has occurred and, if so, sets the damages. One upshot of the risks of high legal costs has been the development of 'no win, no fee' arrangements, whereby a firm of lawyers take on a case on the basis that if they do not win the case, they will not charge any fees to their client. This approach has its pros and cons. The advantage is that an impecunious litigant can take on the case if they can persuade the lawyers of its strength; on the other hand, it means that the lawyers might charge a higher rate than normal in the cases they win, to cover their costs for the number of cases they don't win, thus increasing the cost to the losing party significantly. There is a debate within the UK Government right now regarding whether such arrangements should not be allowed in future.

There have been a lot of UK libel cases based on material that appeared on the internet, for example, on web pages or in e-mails. Part of the reason is that the internet in all its forms, including Web 2.0, affords individuals an opportunity to have their thoughts, often prepared in a rush, published throughout the world. Other reasons are the fact that there are some highly litigious individuals who have decided that electronic criticisms of them are best dealt with by legal action. Normally, it is the person who posted the defamatory statement who is sued. However, an ISP can also be sued if the plaintiff can demonstrate that the ISP was aware that a defamatory statement had gone through its system, yet failed to do anything about it. It may be difficult to identify the person who actually posted the defamatory statement as the person may be hiding behind an anonymous remailer or a pseudonym, or conceivably has 'borrowed' someone else's ID and password. But the ISP is always identifiable and, where necessary, a court order can be obtained forcing it to disclose the IP address of the source of the defamatory statement.

The final reason for the level of libel actions is the fact that in most jurisdictions, the more widely the libel was published the greater the damages. In theory, a libel on the internet can be sent, or forwarded on, to billions of individuals in a very short space of time and at little or no cost to those who post the material. On the other hand, estimating just how many people were likely to have read the particular libellous statement may cause problems for the plaintiff.

Courts will take into account the fact that the internet is a much more informal medium than most print, and therefore a level of flippancy or banter is inevitable. The use of smileys such as ☺ may help indicate the person who made the statement was joking, but this does not necessarily mean they can avoid being sued for defamation. Of course, the defamatory material need not be words. It could be images (such as a computer-manipulated photograph or a cartoon). Needless to say, any ISP or the Web 2.0 service provider will have problems tracking what is being posted through its service, let alone deciding if comments made are defamatory or not.

Case study B

In the *Solicitors from Hell v. The Law Society* case in October 2011, the man behind a consumer website that claims to name and shame allegedly underperforming lawyers lost his slander action against the chief executive of the Law Society. Rick Kordowski, who owns Solicitors from Hell, had sued over a brief exchange between Desmond Hudson of The Law Society and Professor John Flood as they were leaving the BBC studios in July 2011. Flood apparently reported that Hudson had said Kordowski was a criminal. Hudson's case was that he did not say Kordowski was a criminal but that Kordowski's methods of collecting payment to remove comments from the website amounted to criminal behaviour. Striking out the claim, the judge said there was a conflict of evidence and it was impossible for him to say that the defence had no real prospect of success. He added that the alleged wrong was of a relatively low level of seriousness. He concluded that it would not be just to allow the case to proceed, given that the words complained of were spoken to a single person and that there was no evidence of any harm to the plaintiff.

The moral of the story is to consider carefully just how widely the alleged remarks were spread and how much damage the plaintiff might have suffered before starting a defamation action.

By definition, one can only sue for libel if the material that causes damage has been published. Publication is normally assumed to mean that one or more people other than the author of the statement have read the material that causes damage. In a quirk of UK law, which may get changed if the new Defamation Bill gets passed, each time someone new reads or hears the statement it is considered to have been republished. Thus, in the case of a defamatory statement on, say, Wikipedia, it is considered in the UK to have been republished each time someone reads it, and so Wikipedia could find itself the subject of multiple lawsuits based on a single statement. In UK law, the defamation legal action must take place within one year of the publication date. Of course, that one-year period re-starts each time the statement is 'published'. A defamatory statement is presumed in the UK to be false unless the defendant can prove its truth. Even if false, there are still defences available to the person who issued the statement, as we shall see below.

In the USA, with its commitment to freedom of speech, it is much harder to initiate a defamation case, and the defences available to the accused are much broader than in the UK. Thus, in the USA the person first must prove that the material that causes damage was false. Second, that person must prove that the statement caused harm. And, third, they must prove that the statement was made without adequate research into the truthfulness of the statement. However, in the case of a celebrity or public official trying to prove libel, they must not only prove the first three steps, but must also prove that the statement was made with the intent to do harm, or with reckless disregard for the truth, i.e. was made maliciously. Scots law takes a similar approach to this last point. Finally, the USA has the Communications Decency Act, which protects most ISPs and similar organizations from being sued for libel.

Case study C

In November 2011, a US federal appellate court sided with Google in a lawsuit about a bad review of a roofing and construction business. It said that Google was immune from liability for the review, which was authored by an anonymous user. Cal Bay Construction and Castle Roofing sued Google, claiming that an anonymous user defamed them in a post about a leaky roof. Google moved to dismiss the case on the ground that the federal Communications Decency Act protects websites from libel claims that stem from users' comments, and the judge agreed.

In apparent contrast, in a November 2011 UK case, a business owner accused in a Google review of being a paedophile and a thief forced the search giant to remove the entry. A comment by 'Paul' was posted on Google's site about Mr Bennett's business – That Computer Chap – on 26 April 2010. The review said: 'Robbed My RAM and Touched 9 Year Old. What a scam artist, he stole RAM from my computer and replaced it with smaller chips hoping I wouldn't notice and also I later found out touched my 9 year old inappropriately. A Violator and a rogue trader. DO NOT DO TRADE WITH THIS MAN!'

Mr Bennett contacted Google on numerous occasions. The IT consultant, from Bridgnorth in the West Midlands, said that he asked a directory assistance service for a contact number, but when he called it no one answered. Mr Bennett estimated that he has lost 80% of his local business. As a result, he said he had intended to sue Google for defamation. The company later removed the posting. It stated that from time to time it reviews comments flagged as inappropriate.

Defences against a defamation action

Even if a statement is defamatory, there are circumstances in which such statements are permissible in law. First, one can argue (and would have to prove) *that the statement made was true*. However, if the defendant libels the plaintiff and then claims the defence of truth and fails, he may be said to have aggravated the harm. Second, if one cannot prove the statement was true, one can argue that it was *'fair comment' based on facts that are true, or substantially true*. The defendant must show that the words reflect their honestly held opinions, and that the publication was in the public interest (but note that 'the public interest' is not synonymous with 'of interest to the public'). In the UK, the judge decides if the statement was in the public interest or not, and will advise the jury accordingly.

The US Supreme Court has ruled that to win damages in a libel case, the plaintiff must first show that the statements were 'statements of fact or mixed statements of opinion and fact' and second that these statements were false. Conversely, a typical defence to defamation is that the statements are opinion. One of the major tests to distinguish whether a statement is fact or opinion is whether the statement can be proved true or false in a court of law. If the statement can be proved true or false, then, on that basis, the case will be heard by a jury to determine whether it is true or false. If the statement cannot be proved true or false, the court may dismiss the libel case without it ever going to a jury to find facts in the case. This is in marked contrast to the approach in the UK, where a statement containing just opinions is potentially actionable.

The next type of defence is called *privilege*. This defence applies even if the statement made was clearly false. There are two types in the UK; the first is *absolute privilege*, where one cannot even start a defamation case. It covers statements made in a court, made in Parliament by MPs and official reports of either of these – Hansard and official court reports. In contrast, *qualified privilege* is often used by journalists and again refers to the public interest. It would apply to statements made in the media, but could apply elsewhere, for example, to statements made by the police or by someone helping them with their inquiries, or statements made by a fire official, and can cover a report that someone has been expelled from a professional association. Typically, though, one would still have to prove that the statement was not made with malicious intent.

Less common defences include that the claimant *consented* to the dissemination of the statement. Innocent dissemination – the defendant had *no idea that a defamatory statement was being issued through them* – applies in many countries' laws, and on the face of it is a useful defence in the case of a Web 2.0 service, which happens to include defamatory remarks. However, at the moment this approach does not apply in the UK, where anyone involved in the chain of dissemination, for example, in the case of a print publication, the printer, the bookshop or newsagent, the person who delivered the item to an address – though the Post Office is immune – can all potentially get caught up in the action. Similarly, in the Web 2.0 environment, the person or organization that runs the service could well find himself or herself caught up – see Case Study E below.

Another potential defence is provided by the EU's E-Commerce Directive, which has been transposed in to UK law. This provides a defence for an e-commerce service provider against defamation and other actions for illegality if it was simply acting as a postbox, did not influence the contents of what was sent, and did not know, or had no reason to know, that something illegal was being passed through its system. This, in turn, implies that an ISP or Web 2.0 service provider must respond rapidly to any complaint it receives about defamatory messages, as failure to do so would remove this defence from the range of possible defences it could use if sued. I return to this point towards the end of this chapter.

Finally, if all the third parties hearing or reading the statement *do not believe the statement*, there is no damage to the claimant's reputation, so this unusual defence could be tried in such cases.

Possible changes to UK law

At the time this chapter was written, the Defamation Bill had been introduced. One likely outcome is that trials by jury would be abolished for all but exceptional cases involving public figures. This is likely to result in trivial cases being weeded out, and excessive legal costs reduced. The law is also likely to be amended to make it more difficult for large corporations to sue newspapers, by requiring that the plaintiff demonstrate the substantial harm it has suffered. (This is in contrast to current UK law, where the plaintiff merely has to show that harm could occur.).

An interesting suggestion made to the UK Government is that unidentified commentators on blogs and social networks such as Facebook and Twitter should have allegedly defamatory material removed by the service providers if they refuse to reveal their identity. However, the service provider could appeal to a judge against such an order if it felt the material should remain up in the public interest. On the other hand, where the author of allegedly defamatory online material is identifiable, the service will be forced to publish a notice of complaint alongside the article. Only if the service refuses to do so, could it be sued.

The defence of qualified privilege for responsible journalism in the public interest (a common law defence that is not enshrined in formal legislation but by precedent) is likely to be replaced by a new statutory defence. There have also been suggestions that scholarly commentators of what might be called unorthodox science (such as psychic behaviours, homeopathy, chiropractic) should receive greater protection against libel claims made by practitioners of such unorthodox approaches when they criticize the methods and results of these practices.

These changes, if they take place, together with abolition of the rule that each time someone reads an online statement that statement has been republished and so legal action can take place, may help restore some balance to English defamation law, and make it reflect better the realities of the Web 2.0 world. However, as noted above, these are simply possible changes to the law, and a change in the law is unlikely to occur till 2013.

Defamation law in the USA

Defamation law in the USA is much less plaintiff-friendly than its counterparts in other parts of the world. Some states codify what constitutes slander and libel together into the same set of laws. Criminal libel is rare or nonexistent, depending on the state. Defences to libel that can result in dismissal before trial include the statement being one of opinion rather than fact, or being 'fair comment and criticism'. Truth is always a defence.

Most states recognize that some categories of statements are considered to be potentially defamatory *per se*, such that people making a defamation claim for these statements do not need to prove that the statement was defamatory. These categories are:

- accusing someone of a crime
- alleging that someone has a foul or loathsome disease
- adversely reflecting on a person's fitness to conduct their business or trade
- allegations of serious sexual misconduct; in such cases the plaintiff need only prove that someone had published the statement to any third party, no proof of damage is required, though the defendant has defences available, for example, truth.

Across borders and other internet issues

Case study D

On 10 December 2002, the High Court of Australia handed down its judgment in the internet defamation dispute in the case of *Gutnick v. Dow Jones*. The judgment established that internet-published non-Australian publications that defamed an Australian could be held accountable under Australian libel law. A similar case is *Berezovsky v. Forbes* in England. What these cases have confirmed is that something published on a website in country A can still be the subject of a defamation action in country B as long as it was read by people in country B, and the plaintiff enjoyed some reputation in country B. The numbers of readers is important. In one notable English case where it was demonstrated that the only people in the UK who had read the allegedly defamatory statement were the lawyers acting for each side, the judge dismissed the case.

There have been many cases of internet defamation around the world where the person doing the defaming has had to pay significant damages.

Case study E

In 1994 Laurence Godfrey, a British physics lecturer, issued a writ against Phillip Hallam-Baker, who works in the European Particle Physics Centre, claiming damages for libel. The alleged defamation took place on a particular bulletin board. In 1995, Godfrey accepted an undisclosed out-of-court settlement from Hallam-Baker. Godfrey also famously sued Demon Internet, an ISP, when defamatory remarks were posted onto a newsgroup hosted by Demon Internet. Godfrey complained to Demon Internet, but his complaint was ignored. Demon Internet argued that they were innocent disseminators and did not moderate every posting on its service. However, the fact that Godfrey had made a formal complaint demolished that defence.

One general point emerges from the numerous internet-based cases that have been heard. Those in favour of censorship cannot have it both ways. A service that sells itself as a 'family' service, and claims that it uses its software, or human moderators, to delete offensive material is employing a two-edged sword: doing so clearly moves the operator outside the definition of a passive carrier, and the operator of the service must accept that a court will deem it to have assumed the duty of care to which legal liability may attach.

WEB 2.0 POINT

The question of an ISP's or Web 2.0 service's responsibility varies from country to country. However, the general rule is that an ISP or Web 2.0 service provider is likely to be held liable – and therefore at risk of having to pay damages – if it knew, or had good reason to know, that the material broke the law, and could control what passed through its system. Many ISPs make no attempt to control what passes through – they simply offer hardware and software to permit dissemination, and have no effective control over the material. Services that simply send and forward e-mails should be exempt, as would be a body that provides third parties space to set up web pages, messages and so on without exercising any control over them. Mirror sites (exact duplicates of a website at another location, maintained simply to reduce the traffic load on the parent site) will also be exempt.

There are, then, some grey areas. These include companies that do not just provide space, but also advice or consultancy on the design of web pages. Another example is a Web 2.0 service where the service provider moderates in any way the content, for example, deletes inappropriate materials or postings that are out of scope.

So where does that leave the Web 2.0 service? If it turns a blind eye to all content, it may be able to rely on the defence that it did not know, could not have known of the content and did not have effective control over the content. However, if successfully sued once, or indeed if it responded to an earlier complaint by removing a posting, it would then be difficult to argue in any future case that it could not have known that defamatory statements were passing through the system. Alternatively, it could spend time and money with lawyers checking each statement or image and so on posted on the service, not releasing the statement or image and so on until it has been passed, and go quickly out of business. A third choice, to take a random sample of messages to check, seems hardly better. One way to improve its position is for the service to ban anonymous or pseudonymous mailers. It is essential that any Web 2.0 service keeps full records to prove that it did not control content. In addition, the familiar advice already given in this book applies:

- Provide a channel for people to complain about materials posted.
- Withdraw the offending material immediately if a complaint is made.
- Offer to make amends if the complaint is justified, including, if need be, a public apology.
- Make users accept all liability for statements they may make.
- Take out suitable insurance, and one new piece of advice. . .
- Get to know a good libel lawyer.

Conclusions

WEB 2.0 POINT

Ideally, one should not go into the business of running a Web 2.0 service without assessing the legal risks, and ensuring that appropriate insurance cover has been taken out. The laws of libel could potentially lead to the person running the Web 2.0 service and their employer, as well as the individuals who made defamatory statements on the Web 2.0 service, sharing the risk of being sued. The best way to react to a defamatory statement made by a contributor to a Web 2.0 service is to warn the perpetrator of the risks they are taking, and, if necessary, to ensure that person cannot contribute in the future. But that does make the person running the service clearly responsible for the content that is on the Web 2.0 service, with all that this implies.

Everyone who is entitled to use it should be entitled to create and add information to a Web 2.0 operation, and everyone who is a registered user should be entitled to receive information from the service. However, people, whether individuals or corporations, who suffer injury because of defamatory material should be able to obtain compensation from someone if they can prove fault.

What is legal in one country will often be illegal in another. The internet poses fundamental problems for international law, and not just in the fields of law considered in this book. Some lawyers have argued that there should be a separate law of cyberspace, run by a yet to be created international court and developed by the United Nations. Even if agreement could be reached on developing such a body of law and an international court, how it would work and how it could impose its will on individuals based in non-compliant countries is far from clear. I doubt we will see any such developments in the near future.

CHAPTER 7

Cloud computing

Introduction

This chapter is somewhat different in style from other chapters in this book in that it considers a wide range of legal issues that can arise in the use of cloud computing services, whether Web 2.0-related or not. There is no single definition of cloud computing, despite the popularity of the term and of the use of cloud services. Very broadly, a cloud computing service is one that provides computing power of some kind without the installation of content, hardware or software application at the client or customer's premises. Wikipedia defines it as follows:

> Cloud computing provides computation, software, data access, and storage services that do not require end-user knowledge of the physical location and configuration of the system that delivers the services.
>
> Cloud computing describes a new supplement, consumption, and delivery model for IT services based on Internet protocols, and it typically involves provisioning of dynamically scalable and often virtualized resources. It is a byproduct and consequence of the ease-of-access to remote computing sites provided by the Internet. This may take the form of web-based tools or applications that users can access and use through a web browser as if the programs were installed locally on their own computers.
>
> Cloud computing providers deliver applications via the internet, which are accessed from a web browser, while the business software and data are stored on servers at a remote location. In some cases, legacy applications are delivered via a screen-sharing technology, while the computing resources are consolidated at a remote data center location; in other cases, entire business applications have been coded.
>
> Most cloud computing infrastructures consist of services delivered through shared data-centers and appearing as a single point of access for consumers' computing needs. Commercial offerings may be required to meet service-level agreements (SLAs), but specific terms are less often negotiated by smaller companies.

This is a point I return to later in this chapter. Wikipedia continues:

Cloud computing exhibits the following key characteristics:

- **Agility** improves with users' ability to re-provision technological infrastructure resources.
- **Application programming interface** (API) accessibility to software that enables machines to interact with cloud software in the same way the user interface facilitates interaction between humans and computers. Cloud computing systems typically use REST-based APIs.
- **Cost** is reduced and capital expenditure is converted to operational expenditure. This is purported to lower barriers to entry, as infrastructure is typically provided by a third party and does not need to be purchased for one-time or infrequent intensive computing tasks. Pricing on a utility computing basis is fine-grained with usage-based options and fewer IT skills are required for implementation.
- **Device and location independence** enable users to access systems using a web browser regardless of their location or what device they are using. As infrastructure is off-site and accessed via the Internet, users can connect from anywhere.
- **Multi-tenancy** enables sharing of resources and costs across a large pool of users thus allowing for:
  - **Centralization** of infrastructure in locations with lower costs (such as real estate, electricity, etc.)
  - **Peak-load capacity** increases (users need not engineer for highest possible load-levels)
  - **Utilization and efficiency** improvements for systems that are often only 10–20% utilized.
- **Reliability** is improved if multiple redundant sites are used, which makes well-designed cloud computing suitable for business continuity and disaster recovery.
- **Scalability and elasticity** via dynamic ('on-demand') provisioning of resources on a fine-grained, self-service basis near real-time, without users having to engineer for peak loads.
- **Performance** is monitored, and consistent and loosely coupled architectures are constructed using web services as the system interface.
- **Security** could improve due to centralization of data, increased security-focused resources, etc., but concerns can persist about loss of control over certain sensitive data, and the lack of security for stored kernels. Security is often as good as or better than under traditional systems, in part because providers are able to devote resources to solving security issues that many customers cannot afford. However, the complexity of security is greatly increased when data is distributed over a wider area or greater number of devices and in multi-tenant systems that are being shared by unrelated users. In addition, user access to security audit logs may be difficult or impossible. Private cloud installations are

in part motivated by users' desire to retain control over the infrastructure and avoid losing control of information security.

- **Maintenance** of cloud computing applications is easier, because they do not need to be installed on each user's computer.

In 2010, the IT market research company Pew predicted that by 2020 most people would access software and upload and share information using the cloud. Services such as Facebook, Rackspace, Hotmail, Twitter, Yahoo!, YouTube, Flickr, eBay, Google Apps (and all its subsidiary offerings such as Gmail and Google Docs), Amazon EC2, TripAdvisor and Dropbox all either employ the cloud or offer cloud services. This sounds all very promising, but cloud services are not without their legal difficulties, as we shall see. For the moment, one should note three key characteristics of the obligations on a cloud supplier when it enters into a contract with a user: the supplier must maintain the service by keeping its hardware and software operational, must update its hardware and software where necessary, and must keep any third party data passed to it secure.

Some commentators divide up cloud services into a number of subheadings, such as SaaS (software as a service), IaaS (infrastructure as a service), PaaS (platform as a service), StaaS (storage as a service), DaaS (desktop as a service) and so on, but these distinctions are not particularly relevant to the legal issues involved. There is also often a distinction made between a public cloud (a service open to anyone who is willing to sign up to it), a private cloud (as set up by a single organization for internal purposes), a community cloud (open to a closed user group) and a consumer cloud (largely synonymous with public cloud, but refers to services especially aimed at individuals, such as Facebook, Bebo, LinkedIn, Hotmail and Gmail).

Cloud services and their contracts

Whatever the type of cloud service, those who make use of one sign up to a contract (though in the case of the consumer cloud, this is not often made as explicit as it could be). It is important to note the non-negotiable nature of the contracts that most cloud services offer. Consumers and small businesses in general have no scope for negotiation of such licences – it's a case of take it or leave it. Only very large or prestigious organizations have the necessary clout to require a cloud supplier to accept amendments to its standard terms and conditions. There have been a number of surveys carried out of cloud service contracts, which have demonstrated that many of the standard contracts are extremely one-sided in favour of the cloud supplier. A typical example comes from Apple's iCloud service:

You acknowledge and agree that Apple may, without liability to you, access, use, preserve and/or disclose your Account information and Content to law enforcement authorities, government officials, and/or a third party, as Apple believes is reasonably necessary or appropriate, if legally required to do so or if we have a good faith belief that such access, use, disclosure, or preservation is reasonably necessary to: (a) comply with legal process or request; (b) enforce this Agreement, including investigation of any potential violation thereof; (c) detect, prevent or otherwise address security, fraud or technical issues; or (d) protect the rights, property or safety of Apple, its users, a third party, or the public as required or permitted by law.

If the individual or small organization doesn't like the standard terms offered, it has to make a decision whether to risk the standard contract, try another cloud supplier, or give up on cloud services altogether.

Very few cloud service contracts offer guarantees of good service (for example, 100% uptime), and those that offer refunds for poor service availability typically offer such refunds as money off renewal of the subscription rather than a refund of the existing subscription. Some contracts give the service supplier the right to close the service at little or no notice. Indeed, the contracts tend to put obligations on the clients rather than on the service supplier. Few offer automatic encryption of data given to them and/or anonymization of personal data. These days the concept of a privacy impact assessment (PIA) – an independent assessment of the risks to privacy of a particular service – together with advice on how to tighten things up if necessary has become popular. Few of the contracts include references to PIAs. They also do not give clients the ability to check privacy compliance. According to the UK's ICO, *there must be a written contract in place requiring the internet-based service provider to only act on your instructions and to have a level of security equivalent to yours.* Sadly, few of the cloud service supplier contracts offer this level of comfort.

The waiver clauses within cloud service contracts are also problematic. Many cloud service suppliers include a clause by which they exclude all liability for any problems that arise in the service, whether or not it was caused by the service supplier's incompetence or recklessness. Such a contractual clause could be argued over in court if it is a business to business contract, but in the case of a consumer's use of the cloud would probably be declared invalid in UK law under the Unfair Terms in Consumer Contracts Regulations 1999. There is therefore little point in cloud service suppliers including such a clause, and to make things simple, they should amend any liability waiver clause, whether for business or consumers, to read along the lines: 'to the extent permitted by law, we waive all liability'.

Most clients will already have some form of notice and take down policy and procedures on their websites explaining how any third party can complain about content on its website (for example, it infringes copyright or is defamatory). The contract with the cloud service supplier should address the question of how rapidly the cloud supplier can take down offending materials if the client asks it to, but most do not.

Clients may not want their use of the cloud service to be monitored by their cloud service provider. On the other hand, cloud service providers will no doubt wish to monitor use to assess bandwidth and hardware use, for statistical analyses and so on, and indeed some of these statistics could be useful for the client as well. The client should examine the contract to ensure that the terms clearly explain the monitoring carried out, and that it is content with whatever monitoring occurs.

The contract should outline the procedures agreed over deletion of data if and when the contract with the cloud service supplier ends. The client will want to know whether the cloud provider will delete their data on termination. It is likely that the client will want all copies of data in the possession of the cloud provider deleted after it has exercised its rights to have data returned.

Further contractual issues are discussed in various places below.

A slight digression on conflict of law

The concept of 'conflict of laws' is probably as old as established legal systems in the world, and arises where a particular action that is the subject of a legal dispute (perhaps a civil dispute between two individuals, or a criminal case between an individual and the state) has taken place in more than one country. For example, if a contract is made in England but is to be fulfilled abroad, it will be necessary to decide which law governs the validity of the contract. Sometimes the courts must also decide whether or not they have jurisdiction to hear the case, or whether or not to recognize a foreign judgment. Similar issues apply *within* the USA, where one state may have different laws from another.

The issue is particularly acute in the case of cloud services, but had already become problematic with the development of the internet. What if I use my computer in Britain to instruct a computer in another country to send material to another computer in yet another country? What if the material in question breaks laws in some of the countries, but not others? For example, the material may be considered pornographic, copyright infringing, blasphemous, libellous or dangerous to state security in one country, but not in the others. In principle, a country's laws only apply to the territory of that country. Typically, laws are confined to one nation state, or indeed to one region within that nation state. Some laws, such as EU law, in theory apply across all member states, but in practice there are often subtle differences.

In addition, for a law to be effective, it requires some means of enforcement.

This in turn implies that anyone breaking the law must be within reach of the law enforcement apparatus of the nation state.

What conflict of laws issues arise on the web? The real question is: when do they *not* apply? Potentially, every type of problem that is described in this book could involve a conflict of laws. Two types of problem areas can be distinguished. There are those illegal materials where the law of the country makes it an offence to *import* such materials. Thus, in most countries it is an offence to import pornographic materials, or to import copyright infringing materials. In such cases, there is in theory no conflict of law.

Other issues arise when importation is not an offence, but *publication* is, as in defamation. In such cases, the plaintiff may have a choice of where to sue. They may choose to sue in the country where the defamation originated, or to sue in a country or countries of their choice where people are likely to have read the defamatory statements. Judgements have to be made on the attitudes of the courts to defamation law, attitudes to foreign plaintiffs, the size of damages awarded, and the number of readers of the defamatory statements in the country in question. The plaintiff could, if they had deep pockets, take the case to a number of countries' courts.

Physical location is largely irrelevant on the internet. It is not just the case that on the internet no one knows you are a dog. On the internet, *no one knows where the dog is*. One could be anywhere in the world, and indeed could disguise one's location, and still pass information and data to anywhere in the world. Thus, the power of one particular national government to control behaviour becomes weakened. This is especially true as it is incredibly difficult, if not impossible, to police what people are reading on the internet. It is also hard to identify where infringements have occurred or to track the culprits down.

I agree with those who say 'It is a mistake to think of the internet as lawless; all the present laws can and do apply to the internet, and people ignore them at their peril', but the statement overlooks the practical difficulties involved.

Within the EU, there are instruments known as Rome I (covering contracts), and Rome II (covering things such as negligence). These instruments can be helpful in some cases in defining which country's laws will apply if a particular dispute occurs. However, they do not cover every country, or every eventuality, so it has been suggested that new legal principles are required, treating cyberspace as a distinct 'place' legally. Using this approach, we need no longer worry about where the message originated if it originated in cyberspace, and the laws of cyberspace apply. The next logical step is to formulate laws that apply in cyberspace. They will not necessarily be identical to the laws of any given country and, indeed, many of the laws that currently apply in the physical world, such as road traffic offences, would have no counterpart in cyberspace. No one accidentally wanders into cyberspace. They do so deliberately. Once we choose to enter cyberspace, we become subject to its laws. This, in turn, should assist the notion that it is fair to apply laws to those who enter, and may so answer some of the legitimacy questions that currently arise. What should the laws be? Who will set and enforce them? Since they will potentially apply to everyone, there must be international agreement. Certain ground rules can be agreed. For example, there are minimum standards on pornography and defamation that most would subscribe to.

This may all sound naive, but the current situation is potentially such a mess, it is difficult to see any alternative way forward. Governments cannot stop electronic communications entering or leaving their borders, even if they wanted to do so. Nor can they claim the right to impose their system of law on people outside their jurisdiction even if harm has been done to their citizens. It is arrogant to try to monopolize the law in such a way. Unless an agreed body of laws and enforcement appears in cyberspace, governments will inevitably try to police the internet themselves with their own, often inconsistent laws.

Turning now back to the cloud, almost by definition, data stored in the cloud will move from country to country, each with its own laws. In addition, the cloud service supplier may well be based in a different country from that of its clients. The situation becomes particularly problematic when considering the legality of the contract between the cloud service supplier and the client (for example, the differing requirements for 'fairness' of contracts in different countries), and when considering the security of the data held by the cloud service, with 'security' covering issues such as data protection, privacy, and protection of confidential data. If the cloud service includes personal data, there are potentially at least four countries' laws to consider – the home base of the servicer supplier, the home of the client, the country in which an individual whose information is stored is based, and the country where the cloud happens to be residing at any given time.

So which law applies in a cloud dispute? If the dispute relates to a particular contract, typically the contract will define whose law will apply in the case of any dispute – and normally that will be the home country (or state if it's a US-based cloud service operator) of the cloud service. Nonetheless, if the service is to an individual based in the UK, then automatically the Unfair Contract Terms Act 1977 and its associated regulations come into play, irrespective of whether it is mentioned in the contract or not. This provides some minimum guarantees of level of service and liability in cases of negligence or recklessness by the cloud service supplier. There are similar consumer protection laws in some other countries.

Issues of liability can occur, especially with cloud services available to consumers. In general, the law that will apply in such cases will be the law of the country in which the damage occurred, though there are some exceptions in unusual circumstances.

In the case of data protection, the law is on the face of it clear: if the data was held in the UK, or if control of the data was based in the UK, then the UK DPA applies. This has significant implications, as we shall see below.

Information security, data protection and the cloud

Numerous surveys of users and potential users of cloud services have demonstrated concerns about the security of data, for example, hacking, and data protection as an inhibitor to the use of cloud services. The key risks are seen as the exposure of confidential and personal information to governments, competitors, thieves or opportunists.

The cloud's ubiquitous and dynamic nature means that data provided to a cloud service supplier will move from country to country without the client knowing when or where the data is being moved. Furthermore, the data might well be backed up or replicated in multiple countries. Indeed, it is possible that more than one cloud service supplier co-operate with each other and transfer data between their servers. However, the laws against computer misuse and data protection laws vary greatly from country to country, with some countries offering no realistic protection at all in their legislation.

UK data protection law defined a data controller as the person making decisions about the use of the personal data. Now, other than where the cloud service supplier is keeping its own database of client details, normally that would be the cloud service client who is passing data that happens to be personal data (for example, the names of senders and recipients of e-mails) to the cloud service for processing. However, there could well be circumstances where, for example, the cloud service rather than the cloud client decides movement of personal data from one country to another. In such cases, arguably it is the cloud service that is the data controller, and therefore carries responsibilities under data protection legislation. If this doesn't apply (and it must be said that the law is a bit ambiguous about whether a cloud service is a data controller or not in these circumstances), then in law, the cloud service supplier is a 'data processor' – someone who is handling personal data under the instructions of a data controller.

Of course, it is quite possible in some set-ups for the cloud service client to be (either known or unknown to them) dealing with more than one cloud service. This adds to the complexity of the situation. A data processor is obliged to be tied to the data controller in law. Specifically, the data controller (the cloud service client) is obliged to impose on the data processor (the cloud service) an obligation to abide by the 7th Principle of the DPA, the one requiring that appropriate methods are employed to avoid any accidental loss, destruction or unauthorized disclosure of personal data. There should be wording along these lines in the contract between the cloud service supplier and its client:

The cloud service supplier agrees and warrants that it has in place appropriate technical and organisational measures to protect all personal data as defined in the Data Protection Act 1998 against accidental or unlawful loss, destruction, alteration, unauthorised disclosure or access, and all other forms of unlawful processing in accordance with the Act. The cloud service supplier further agrees and warrants that it will take all necessary steps to ensure compliance with those measures, and to ensure the reliability of any employees or agents who have access to the personal data, and in particular will ensure that all such persons shall receive appropriate training in data protection, security and the care of personal data. The supplier shall supply the client with a statement of the technical and organisational measures adopted to meet its obligations together with a statement of the steps taken to ensure the reliability of any employees or agents who will have access to the personal data. If at any time the supplier becomes aware of a breach of the required standards or is not able to deliver compliance with the required standards, it shall promptly inform the client, and the client shall be entitled to suspend the processing of the relevant personal data by the supplier, and to demand a pro rata refund of any fees already paid or due to cover the period of suspension.

Failure to impose this, or something similar, in a contract between the cloud service supplier and its client means a UK-based client (as data controller) has broken the law. Furthermore, the contract should include provision for the cloud service supplier to pay compensation to individuals, or any fine payable to the Information Commissioner, should a breach of the DPA result from the cloud service supplier's own failings. In addition, the DPA provides the Information Commissioner with the powers to impose enforcement notices and information notices on a data controller. The former require the data controller to do something, while the latter requires the data controller to provide information on some aspect of the processing of personal data that has gone on. The contract with the cloud service supplier must ensure that the cloud service responds rapidly to either requirement.

It is important to note that the DPA kicks in either when the data controller is UK based, or if the data is resident in the UK, even for a short period of time. This means that if a cloud service supplier, which is based in (say) the USA, concludes a deal with a US client, but one of the servers it uses from time to time to hold the data happens to be in the UK, the UK DPA applies to the processing of that data. This will no doubt come as a surprise to all the parties involved, and may not be of great significance in practice, but nonetheless, both parties should be made aware of this possibility.

A UK-based organization should, incidentally, check its notification that it has sent to the ICO if it decides to use the cloud. It could be that the countries where the data might be sent to, and the uses made of the data will change as a result of the cloud service, and the law requires that the ICO should be informed of any such changes.

As has been made clear in this book, the UK's DPA makes it a breach of the Act to transfer personal data to a country without adequate data protection laws unless the transfer is necessary for a contract, has the explicit approval of the individual, or for a few other restricted reasons. Most cloud service providers are US-based, though some have UK or other EU-based subsidiaries. Those that are US-based often commit to safe harbour principles – that data in their care will be placed in a physical environment where UK (or EU) data protection laws are complied with. However, not all commit to this, and it would be a very strange cloud service that committed to never letting data under its control outside the EEA. Those that do not commit to a safe harbour are therefore particularly high risk from a client's point of view, as the data may well be held in a country with little or no regard for data protection laws. Rather worryingly, some of the biggest cloud service suppliers do not commit in their contracts either to follow EU data protection laws, or to place client data in a safe harbour. Furthermore, the contracts do not oblige the cloud service supplier to inform a client if a search warrant has been issued to inspect the data the service holds.

Even if the cloud service supplier promises – ideally in a formal contract, which specifies the safe harbour principles it follows – to maintain the data it is entrusted with in a safe harbour, how can one be sure the data will stay in a safe harbour when the entire business rationale for cloud is to place the data in whatever is the economically most advantageous place? The whole point is that the data should be kept in whatever data centre is available, and may only stay there a short time before being moved on to another data centre. One approach to this potential problem is to get the cloud service supplier to agree to use a safe harbour combined with a 'if anything goes wrong you will be subject to the rules of the European data protection law' contractual obligation. Then, if anything did go wrong, the supplier would be penalized as if they were operating within the EEA. But, as is noted elsewhere in this chapter, cloud service suppliers are notoriously unwilling to negotiate on contractual terms. Nonetheless, it is strongly recommended that a potential client demand that basic safe harbour principles be applied. These are:

- *Notice* – Individuals must be informed that their data is being collected and about how it will be used.
- *Choice* – Individuals must have the ability to opt out of the collection and forward transfer of the data to third parties.
- *Onward transfer* – Transfers of data to third parties may only occur to other organizations that follow adequate data protection principles.

- *Security* – Reasonable efforts must be made to prevent loss of collected information.
- *Data integrity* – Data must be relevant and reliable for the purpose it was collected for.
- *Access* – Individuals must be able to access information held about them, and correct or delete it if it is inaccurate.
- *Enforcement* – There must be effective means of enforcing these rules.
- *Certification* – The cloud service must re-certify every 12 months. It can either perform a self-assessment to verify that it complies with these principles, or hire a third party to perform the assessment.

Finally, *appropriate employee training* and *effective dispute mechanisms* should be in place.

One particular area of concern is the Uniting and Strengthening America by Providing Appropriate Tools Required to Intercept and Obstruct Terrorism Act, better known as the Patriot Act. This is a wide-ranging piece of legislation that allows US authorities to compel, among others, ISPs to disclose information about their customers and without those customers knowing that such information has been requested. Despite the Act's title, its use can extend beyond terrorism to any criminal investigation. Because of its wide-ranging powers, this Act has been viewed with distaste by those countries with well developed data protection legislation in place, and has led to some governments (for example, Canada and The Netherlands) banning organizations under their control from passing any data to US-based organizations, and has allegedly led to Amazon delaying the launch of its new Kindle Fire within the EU because of the incompatibility of the Patriot Act with EU data protection legislation.

The key issue for a cloud service client, therefore, is not just whether the cloud service offers a safe harbour for its information, but also whether it wishes to take the risk that its data might end up in the hands of US authorities as a result of a Patriot Act action. In particular, an informed judgement should be made if particularly sensitive personal data or commercially confidential data is involved. It is one of many risk factors one should take into account when engaging a cloud service supplier. The Patriot Act is not alone; there are similar pieces of legislation in other countries where cloud data might be held, but they are generally not as far-reaching or as well known as the Patriot Act.

Finally, the client may well have rules regarding the length of time personal data is retained. How these retention rules are complied with when the data is hosted and processed in the cloud needs to be clarified in the contract with the cloud provider.

Security issues are also a major concern. There have been instances when one cloud service client was able to read another cloud service client's materials. A prospective client of a cloud service therefore should undertake appropriate due diligence about the service to ensure that security is at a level appropriate to the value and/or sensitivity of the information being loaded onto the cloud. It is also a good idea to test the cloud service first with non-sensitive information. I recommend that the contract with the cloud service supplier be negotiated if possible to include a clause obliging the service to comply with certain specified international security standards, and/or with the client's own security standards. The contract should make explicit the service provider's liability (and limits of liability) in case of data loss or a security breach. A good service supplier will accept liability for direct costs, but will resist the idea of compensating for consequential loss, such as loss of goodwill or reputation of the client because of data loss or a security breach. Clients should resist any contract that absolves the cloud service from any liability for data loss or security breach.

Other legal issues

Data protection and security of data are not the only legal issues that can arise. Questions might arise regarding who is responsible if the data offered by a client is somehow amended or released resulting in an illegality, such as *defamation* or *breaking national security laws*. As noted above, it is not clear what country's laws might apply in such cases. In current UK law, a cloud service supplier might find itself caught up in a defamation action, because it helped the defamation along. If the cloud provider neither monitors the content on its site, nor responds to complaints, it is likely to be caught up in such an action. While it is unrealistic to expect the cloud service supplier to monitor everything on its servers (and indeed, this could be problematic from a privacy point of view), it is reasonable to expect it to respond to complaints received regarding alleged defamatory comments. The contract between the client and the cloud service supplier will probably require a warranty and indemnity relating to defamatory statements. As noted elsewhere in this book regarding defamation, there is also potential protection for cloud service suppliers who act as 'mere hosts' under the EU E-Commerce Directive.

It is also unclear who owns the *database rights* to data collected in the cloud, especially if some of the data is metadata added by the cloud service supplier.

Software licences, copyright licences and *database rights licences* are also potentially problematic. If a client has permission to use a particular software or database 'on site', does that include 'in the cloud'? A licence might state that the material must not be sent to another country. Such geographical limitations in licences are not uncommon, and are often predicated on the fact that sales executives depend heavily on commission earned for sales in their country, and get no benefit from sales in another country that grant permission to use in their home country. Such restrictions may even go further, stating that a particular database or software may only be used on a single computer, or may only be used by employees of the licensee, or comes with warranties that it does not infringe any UK laws, but provides no such warranties for outside the UK. If such databases and/or software are going to be placed in the cloud, these licences will have to be renegotiated. Many licensors are now aware of the cloud and are willing to be flexible on this matter. If they are not, then a decision has to be taken whether to place that database or software on the cloud, or to use an alternative database or software that imposes no such restrictions.

Cloud service providers often include in their contract terms and conditions a term that the client grants the provider a licence to republish some or all of the client's data for the purpose of provision of the service. The client should ensure that the extent of any licence is:

- limited to what is necessary for the provision of the cloud computing service
- compatible with the client's obligations under the DPA to process data fairly and lawfully and for limited stated purposes
- compatible with its obligations to third parties.

Finally, cloud service clients should ensure that the contract confirms that the ownership of copyright and other IPRs in materials passed by the client at any time to the service remain with the original owners, and is not assigned to the cloud service.

Freedom of information could also be an issue for public authorities. A provider of remote computing services is likely to be regarded as holding information on behalf of a public authority for the purposes of FoI; this is not an area normally covered in standard service terms and conditions. The question then arises whether the information will be both available when it is needed and unchanged from the original. If a cloud service provider uses the public authority's data, say to create a new document, could it be argued that the new document is held on behalf of the authority? All of this would have to be resolved in the contract between the public authority and the cloud service supplier. Furthermore, the details of the contract (excluding costs of the deal) between a public authority and a provider of cloud services itself might of course be itself subject to disclosure in response to a FoI request, and both parties need to be aware of this possibility.

Finally, *trademark* issues can arise if someone uses a third party trademark 'in the course of trade' without permission. In this regard, cloud services are no different from any other body that uses trademarks in the course of business. The question of the liability of a cloud service supplier that allows one of its clients to promote goods and services and in doing so infringes a third party trademark has never been tested in court, but it is likely that the contract between the service supplier and the client will indemnify the service supplier against any such infringements.

Questions to ask a cloud service supplier before you sign up
Here is a list of questions that could be asked of any cloud service supplier before signing their contract:

• Who (both within and outside the service supplier) will be able to see my information?
• Who owns and controls your infrastructure? Is this outsourced to any third party?
• Where are the infrastructure elements located? (Check what data protection apply in those countries; if the answer is 'unknown countries', it is best not to sign up to that cloud supplier.)
• Can I see a copy of your reliability reports (if any)?
• What service levels are guaranteed? (for example, availability, time to resolve a problem) and what compensation do you offer if you fail to fulfil that? (In particular, clients should resist discounts on future subscriptions, but insist where possible to receive financial compensation there and then and/or the right to terminate early with refunds.)
• Have you ever had security breaches or loss of service in the past?
• What happens if there is a loss of service? Do I have a contact name?
• Will you abide by the DPA when you handle my information?
• Will you pay damages if a breach of the Act occurs that is your fault?
• What happens if my data is lost? Do I have a contact name?
• How easy would it be to migrate my data to a competitor service once this contract ends? Can you guarantee that it will be in a usable format?
• Who is responsible for ID management and access control?
• What are the names of your employees responsible for handling our data?
• What security policies, technology and systems do you employ? What national or international standards do they comply with?
• What compensation is there for service or other failure by you?
• Is the contract negotiable?
• Do I get any rights of refusal before you make changes to the service that affect my data? (Alternatively, can we cancel early and get money back if we cancel early because of unwanted service changes?)
• Will you use my organization's name or type of data given to you on any of your advertising? (If need be, require that the cloud supplier has to ask for permission each time.)
• What special measures will you take regarding data we tag as confidential?
• Could we have a free trial with some non-sensitive data before committing ourselves?
• (For public authorities only) Are you aware of, and will you abide by, the possible implications of the Freedom of Information Act?

- Are you willing to include clauses in the contract relating to ensuring there is no unauthorized loss or destruction of data?
- What assurances can you give that data protection standards will be maintained in a country with weak, or no, data protection laws, or where government inspection powers are very wide-ranging?
- Can you provide us with routine backups of all our data stored on your cloud?
- Will you guarantee to inform us if you become aware of any data security breach that affects or involves our data?

These questions are not just necessary for the client's own reassurance; in some cases, they, and their answers, should be documented to comply with requirements of the DPA. Some of these questions may well be answered in the draft contract or in documents published by the service. For the others, you should be willing to sign a non-disclosure agreement with the cloud service supplier before receiving answers. Some of the answers you should press to be included in the contract itself; you should not allow yourself to be satisfied with informal assurances. The real issue in using cloud services is that you are entering into a relationship on standard terms and conditions, with limited information about how the service is provided and little power to negotiate. You need faith in the provider to be comfortable with that position. However, the types of answers (or the refusal to provide answers) to the questions above should help justify (or not) that faith.

In October 2011, the French data protection authority announced a public consultation on cloud computing. It seeks to gather opinions from stakeholders on cloud computing services for businesses, to identify legal and technical solutions that address data protection concerns while taking into account the economic interests involved. It addresses several specific topics about personal data protection in the cloud computing context, including:

- cloud computing providers as data processors
- applicable law (what law applies to cloud computing stakeholders?)
- regulation of data transfers (for example, what legal instruments are best suited to regulate cloud computing? Would binding corporate rules for data processors be an appropriate legal mechanism for transferring personal data to cloud computing service providers?)
- data security (for example, cloud-specific risks and proposed security measures).

It is clear that I am not the only person with concerns! But I would conclude that one should not get paranoid about the cloud. It offers many potential benefits. One should enter into a cloud contract being aware of both the benefits and the risks.

CHAPTER 8

Liability

Introduction

Liability can be broadly defined as a legal duty or obligation, or, slightly more specifically in the context of this book, the duty of care an individual or an organization owes to another. Failure in that duty means that the person who suffers as a consequence can sue the person or organization for the damage caused. It is important to note that the law of liability differs significantly between different countries. The focus of this chapter will be on UK law. In the UK, liability issues can arise both in contracts, and under the law of tort. This is not necessarily the case in other countries.

Contracts

The law of contract is complex and details of it are outside the scope of this book. Readers interested in studying this topic further are recommended to read a standard text on the topic, such as Paul Richards' *Law of Contract* (10th edn, Pearson, 2011) or other texts as listed in Chapter 9. Readers should also note that the law of Scotland differs from that in England and Wales in some regards. In a nutshell, a contract is an agreement between two parties. Such an agreement can be verbal, as when one buys some fruit from a greengrocer, but the sorts of contracts that readers are likely to encounter in their professional lives, such as licences for the delivery of electronic resources, are in writing. They must involve an offer of something, for example, permission to access, display and download electronic resources, and an acceptance of that offer, typically indicated by the signing of the contract. Contracts do not have to involve money changing hands, though often they do. Any 'consideration' that is valuable to the other party is enough to make the contract legally secure, such as a promise to do something for the other party, or indeed, in some rare cases, a promise *not* to do something.

The important issue in contracts as far as liability is concerned is the fact that the supplier of goods or services *must* use reasonable skill and care in the provision of these services or goods. This applies whether or not the contract is written or verbal, and whether or not money changes hands. This is a good example of an *implied term*, which, if there is some sort of dispute between the parties, the courts will recognize as having been implied even if they were not explicitly stated. Some implied terms can be deduced from the actions of the parties, but others are in a sense imposed by the courts on the parties whether they like it or not. The requirement that the party supplying a service or goods must use reasonable skill and care in doing so is an example of the latter type of implied contractual term. It is not just the courts, however, that have chosen to require a reasonable duty of skill and care on those party to a contract; in some cases this is also built into legislation. Thus, UK law imposes the following implied terms:

- In every contract for the sale of goods it is implied that the seller has the right to sell the goods, and the purchaser has the right to enjoy possession of the goods without being harassed by any third party.
- In every contract for the sale of goods it is implied that the goods correspond to the description of them provided by the seller, and that they are of adequate quality (though this latter point does not apply to sales between two individuals).
- Turning to contracts for the supply of services, the law requires that the person providing the service shall do so with reasonable care and skill; this is the key component of the law as far as users of electronic information services, including Web 2.0 applications, are concerned.
- There is also an implied term, imposed by statute, that the service shall be supplied in reasonable time.

Tort

Quite separate from contract is the concept of tort. This can be defined as a wrongful act or omission whereby the person who suffered damage can sue, and where there was no contract between the parties. It provides compensation for personal injury or damage caused by a third party's negligence, though passing off (see Chapter 3) and defamation (see Chapter 6) are also classed as torts. In essence, this is about individuals or organizations owing a duty of care to each other, even though they have no contractual relationship and, indeed, may not have even been aware of each other before the tort occurred.

The law of tort on uses of Web 2.0 comes down to this: if someone causes damage or loss because of their negligence or recklessness, the person suffering that damage or loss can sue them. However, the injured party must demonstrate that they owed a duty of care, that this duty was breached, the damage resulted from the breach, and that this could have been reasonably foreseen. So how might such an event arise in the context of Web 2.0? Most probably because of inaccurate or misleading information or instructions provided to the user.

Quality of electronic information

It is no secret that the quality of information to be found on the internet is variable. Arguably, that is also true of the quality of information to be found on intranets as well. Little has been done on providing quality markers on items found electronically, and indeed it is difficult to see how, with the volume and heterogeneity of the materials available, that could be achieved, but users are given valuable clues from the provenance of the material, from recommendations by others, from the authorship and so on. It would be difficult to argue the case for tort if one relied on a source of information taken from an unknown source on the internet, though one might be able to sue for damage caused by malware, such as computer viruses, that resulted from the supplier's negligence or deliberate actions – assuming one can track who the supplier was and assuming they are based in a jurisdiction where they can be sued.

One thing is for sure – courts will be much more sympathetic to a complainant if they had to pay for the information than if they got the information for nothing. But that does not mean that a provider of free information can be as reckless or as negligent as they like. And it doesn't just apply to the information content itself; typographical errors, gaps in coverage, poor metadata or indexing could also lead to loss or damage. The problem is particularly acute where the information being supplied is professional, whereby significant decisions might be taken as a result of receiving that information, for example, financial advice, legal information (including this book!), patent information, medical information or engineering information. (It is for this reason that you are warned that the contents of this book do *not* represent formal legal advice, and that if you have any legal queries relating to the issues raised in this book, you should seek the guidance of a lawyer.)

Timeliness may also be an issue in some cases; out of date information can be as dangerous as inaccurate information. But in all these cases, the courts would expect an information user to use common sense, for example, they should not rely on just one uncertain source, and/or they should use their own experience and common sense when applying the information they have learned from the electronic resource. In other words, the user, too, must use reasonable skill and judgement when evaluating the information provided to them.

Exercise 1

A Web 2.0 service offering cookery tips recommends that a particular mushroom is particularly tasty and can be picked in woodlands for subsequent cooking. A photo of the mushroom is shown. Unfortunately, the particular mushroom, *Hypholoma sublateritium*, is confusingly similar in appearance to *Hypholoma fasiculare*, which is poisonous. Someone following the advice of the site picks some of the latter, and is hospitalized as a result. Can the patient sue the Web

2.0 site? And if so, who do they sue – the owner of the site, or the person who suggested picking the mushrooms?

In any case, courts will rarely offer compensation for consequential losses, and tend to only compensate for the direct loss suffered. Thus, for example, if because of inaccurate train timetable information a train you thought you were catching for a job interview was not running and you missed the train, and thereby missed the interview, you could probably sue the train company for the cost of the train ticket, but not for the consequential loss of any pay rise had you got the job.

Waiver clauses

Waiver clauses are beloved of all suppliers of electronic information. Typical wording, taken from Lynette Owen's *Clark's Publishing Agreements: a book of precedents* (8th edn, Bloomsbury Professional, 2010), looks like this:

> Whilst Publisher will use all reasonable skill and care in the creation and supply of the service and the data, Publisher does not give any warranty as to its suitability, accuracy or fitness for any purpose. Publisher excludes all liability whether in contract, tort (including liability for negligence) or otherwise for the suitability, accuracy or fitness for any purpose of the service and any data, and limits its liability for any other liability under this Agreement to the fees payable by you for the element of the service or data in dispute. Publisher excludes all liability for loss of business revenue or profits, anticipated savings or wasted expenditure, corruption or destruction of data, or for any indirect or consequential loss whatsoever. Save as expressly permitted in this agreement, all warranties, conditions or other terms implied by statute, common law or otherwise are excluded to the fullest extent permitted by law.

Owen comments, '[P]ublishers are not alone in wanting to limit their potential liability, so licensors should not be surprised when licensees seek to make elements of this clause mutual. . . the suitability and enforceability of any such clause needs careful consideration.' This understates the situation. Licensees are increasingly not only demanding that publishers cannot use such clauses, but are also attempting to require publishers to confirm that the materials they supply are not defamatory, or break any laws, such as those relating to contempt of court, incitement to terrorism, pornography and so on. Furthermore, if an electronic publisher were reckless or negligent in the way information was presented and delivered to clients, a court would be unlikely to accept that such a clause represents the last word on the situation.

Nonetheless, many electronic licence agreements are presented to clients on a take it or leave it basis. In other words, they are not agreements to be negotiated, as life would be too complex, and too much time would be wasted on individual negotiations, and it would be difficult for an electronic publisher to manage a large number of clients, each of whom has subtly different contractual relationships with the electronic publisher.

Case study A

PATCHETT AND PATCHETT V. SWIMMING POOL AND ALLIED TRADES ASSOCIATION (2009)

The Swimming Pool and Allied Trades Association (SPATA) is the trade body for swimming pool installers. It escaped liability for information on its website that suggested a company was financially robust when it was not. The plaintiffs, the Patchetts, had ordered a swimming pool, relying on SPATA website's assurances about Crown Pools Ltd. Crown Pools became insolvent, and the Patchetts lost the money they had paid, and did not get the job done. They sued SPATA, claiming its website had misled them.

Using Google, Mr Patchett came across the website of SPATA in his search to engage an appropriate contractor. SPATA is a well established, incorporated trade association and its members include most of the major swimming pool installers in the UK. From the website, Mr Patchett obtained the names and contact details of three of its members. Of the three, a quotation from Crown Pools was obtained and accepted and the works duly commenced.

The website claimed that Crown was a member of SPATA, that SPATA members have high standards, that Crown had been checked for creditworthiness and the quality of its work, and that Crown was a member of SPATA's unique bond and warranty scheme. Furthermore, it stated that this scheme offered 'customers peace of mind that their installation will be completed fully to SPATA Standards – come what may!'

The Patchetts claimed that they relied on the representations on the website by choosing Crown Pools and entering into the contract. As it happened, the representations were untrue. Crown Pools was only an affiliate member of SPATA and as such was not covered by the bond and warranty scheme. The Patchetts claimed damages of approximately £44,000 as a result of SPATA's breach of duty to take reasonable care in making these representations.

The Court felt that while SPATA no doubt knew that the representations on their website would likely be acted on, it would not expect consumers to do so without further enquiry. The website had clearly stated that an information pack, including a contract checklist setting out questions for potential installers, was available on the website. The Patchetts admitted they had read this advice, but had not ordered the information pack (though in fact the information pack did not add that much more to what the Patchetts already knew).

The Court decided that it would not be fair for SPATA to assume a legal responsibility for the accuracy of the statements on the website without the consumer inquiring further, which the website itself encouraged.

Furthermore, SPATA had not given a warranty that Crown Pools was at all times creditworthy, but rather that its financial record and previous work had been checked in the past and had been up to SPATA standards. Nonetheless, the judgment here was a bit odd. One judge assumed that every consumer reads every page of a website; the advice about the information pack was not on the home page, but on the 'about us' page, a page that could easily be ignored. Ironically, if the Patchetts *had* ordered the information pack, they would have almost certainly won their case, even though the pack would not have given them enough information to question Crown Pools' financial strength.

Other court cases

The key message from this, and indeed other court cases, is that consumers must check all information obtained from the internet. Websites need to be read as a whole and where the website encourages further information to be obtained, consumers should do so. The key message for providers of electronic information is that a well worded disclaimer or recommendation to seek further advice before committing oneself is important in reducing the duty of care that an electronic publisher has towards its readers.

There are a number of classic cases all over the world that emphasize the need for care when reading and interpreting information supplied, although if the information appears to be authoritative, and if the consumer of that information is likely not to fully understand the subject, the duty of care on the publisher is that much higher. So to some extent, it depends on the nature of the information and the consumers of it.

Case study B

In *Saloomey v. Jepperson*, a US court case, the widow of a pilot of a light aircraft killed in a crash sued the publishers of electronic sat-nav-type guides to airfields for owners of private aircraft because the instructions given failed to identify a hill in the way of the glide path for landing. The publisher claimed the pilot had a responsibility to be aware of his surroundings and should not have solely relied on the electronic instructions, but the court decided the publisher was liable.

In contrast, a French case involved a medical text that gave the wrong dosage for administering a drug, and the doctor relying on it was sued but claimed the publisher was the one at fault. The courts decided that the doctor should have used their professional judgement, and so the doctor was found liable, not the publisher. A notable Australian case, *Greenmoss v. Dun & Bradstreet*, centred on a misleading report by Dun & Bradstreet that Greenmoss was in financial difficulty when it was not (an ironic alternative to the swimming pool case above!). In this case, Greenmoss, the company, won its case. Dun & Bradstreet is a US company, but the case was heard in an Australian court.

Misleading information

It isn't just misleading information that a publisher has to worry about. Any electronic publishers might also find themselves in difficulty because of the illegal nature of the content that their publication carries. There is no carte blanche that one can publish what one likes – this has always been limited to a greater or lesser extent by the authorities anxious to prevent the dissemination of materials that are thought to be contrary to the country's social, political or economic good. A major problem for anyone who publishes materials electronically, however, is that the law is not consistent between one country and another. Thus, for example, an image of a scantily clad woman might not attract any difficulties in the USA or UK, but might well do so in Saudi Arabia. The major classes of controversial content are:

- pornography and other sexually explicit materials
- material encouraging or showing violence
- defamatory materials
- materials that interfere with the administration of justice
- materials that encourage terrorism, or to overthrow the state or the current political order
- materials that encourage race hatred or other tensions between groups in society
- materials that reveal official secrets
- materials that infringe copyright, database rights and other IPRs
- materials that damage others' computers, for example, viruses
- bulk mailings, for example, spam
- anything that threatens the privacy of individuals
- materials that reveal commercial or trade secrets
- any harassment of another person, for example, cyberstalking or posting abusive messages, or encouraging others to do so
- materials designed to encourage fraud.

And more! But as noted above, different countries take different approaches or view these various types of material with different levels of seriousness. This puts the publisher of electronic materials in an almost impossible position, as they cannot possibly know the formal letter of the law, let alone how it is used in practice, in every country of the world where the information is likely to be distributed or read.

WEB 2.0 POINT

Those who tweet or post messages on Facebook can easily find themselves on the wrong side of the law. For example, in a recent high profile murder case in the UK, someone tweeted during the trial damaging information about the defendant. Had those tweets been read by any of the jury, it could well have biased their decision on the verdict. The person who did the tweeting was almost certainly in contempt of court, and, had the defendant been found not guilty, could have been the defendant himself in a defamation action.

Another example relates to the riots that occurred in a number of UK cities in August 2011. Several individuals were found guilty of encouraging or inciting riots in their locality by posting messages on Facebook. They have been sentenced to long terms of imprisonment. When they appealed, the Court of Appeal noted 'the abuse of modern technology for criminal purposes includes incitement of many people by a single step'.

The key point is that Web 2.0 users should think carefully about what they post, forward or re-tweet before doing so. In a recent UK survey, about a third of the public stated that they believed anyone who posted on a Web 2.0 service should adhere to the same journalistic standards as are imposed by the UK's Press Complaints Commission. Although sometimes ignored by journalists themselves, the standards do require a level of care before publishing stories.

Employers' liability

As if all this wasn't enough, employers are often deemed to be liable for actions carried out by their employees, even if what the employee did was against the employer's rules. However, the liability only occurs when the employee did something – for example, posted a defamatory message on a social networking site – which was part of the employee's normal duties (this in part explains why so many employers ban the use of social networking sites during work hours by employees). One fact that has to be borne in mind is that the employer is often easier to identify than the employee in question, and has more funds available if it is a case of suing for damages. For these reasons, not merely should employers have suitable rules regarding disciplinary offences, but they should also implement those rules (there is no point in saying uploading pornography is a disciplinary offence if then an employee who does this does not then get formally disciplined) and should put in place training programmes to explain the background to these rules and the consequences of breaking them.

Employers *may* also wish to adopt an approach of randomly checking the contents of employees' desktop and laptop equipment that is employer-owned. The routine or random checking of employees' incoming and outgoing e-mails as well as desktop contents is problematic. The law in the UK is strict on who is allowed to intercept electronic communications, or to carry out covert surveillance, and for what reasons. The topic is outside the scope of this book. Readers interested in this aspect of employer liability are advised to check the Regulation of Investigatory Powers Act 2000 and associated legislation, and commentary on that legislation.

A model contract for those submitting user-generated content?

One way of reducing the risks of being found liable for content found on a Web 2.0 service including user-generated content is to impose contractual rules on anyone submitting such content. The following contract is based on one provided by Williams, Calow and Lee, *Digital Media Contracts* (Oxford University Press, 2011):

1. We encourage all our users to interact with this site and to submit materials to the site. To ensure that this is done safely and lawfully, we have established the rules set out below.
2. Unless you and we agree otherwise, you confirm that you own (or have an explicit licence that grants you permission to submit the material onto our site) the copyright and all other applicable intellectual property rights in the user-generated content that you submit, and that you will continue to own (or hold the explicit licence) for the lifetime of the copyright or other intellectual property rights concerned.
3. You confirm that you grant us a free of charge, non-exclusive indefinite licence to put your user-generated content on our site, on our partner sites (if any) and that you grant us permission to reproduce all or part of your user-generated content in any medium existing now or developed in the future. Please do not submit material that you would not like to be used in this way. Please also note that if a third party without permission copies your user-generated content from our site, it is up to you to take any legal action you think appropriate.
4. By submitting your user-generated content, you grant us all the rights necessary to enable the distribution of your user-generated content, including the right to adapt or amend the material where necessary for these purposes.
5. You further confirm that (a) the user-generated content you submit has not been copied from someone else or does not include any third party

materials, unless you have obtained the necessary licence that grants you permission to pass said material to us; (b) you have the permission of all people involved in the making of the user-generated content, or appearing in it; (c) that you have explained to all people involved in making the material or appearing in it how this user-generated content will be used and disseminated, and have obtained their specific consent to such use; and (d) that if anyone involved in the making of the material, or appearing in it is under 18, then their parents or lawful guardians have given the necessary consent

6. You further confirm that the content of the user-generated content you submit is lawful and suitable, and does not break any laws relating to pornography, defamation, intellectual property rights, data protection, privacy, contempt of court, terrorism, race hatred or official secrets. You further confirm that the content does not include anything that could cause any third party physical or financial damage, or which in our reasonable opinion could bring us into disrepute, or which in our reasonable opinion would be considered to be spam, spyware, computer viruses or Trojans, or anything that encourages fraud.

7. You confirm that you will not use our site to threaten or harass anyone else, to impersonate anyone else, or otherwise use the site in a way that is anti-social or unlawful.

8. We reserve the right to review your user-generated content before adding it to the site. If we determine that your user-generated content does not comply with these rules, we reserve the right to stop it being made available on the site, and remove the user-generated content and/or links to it from the site at any time and without prior notice to you.

9. At all times, you remain responsible for the user-generated content you post.

10. If anything in these rules is not clear to you, or if you think that other content breaches these rules, please contact us at. . .

Use of such wording, or something similar, will not necessarily get the provider of a Web 2.0 service off the legal hook, but should help enormously in both warning contributors of their responsibilities and demonstrating an awareness of the problems Web 2.0 poses.

WEB 2.0 POINT
Web 2.0 services by and large refuse to accept responsibility for the content uploaded by their users, so if you upload anything that is illegal in any way, or can cause damage to third parties, the responsibility will typically be yours alone. There may be a case in some circumstances for arguing that there is joint liability between the person who posted the materials and the Web 2.0

service, but even then, the person who posted the material remains liable. It is therefore very important to ensure that nothing you post breaks any law or can cause damage to third parties.

Conclusions

This chapter has just given a flavour of some of the liability issues that can arise, for individuals and/or their employers when posting materials onto a Web 2.0 service or running such a service. In essence, one should be just as careful when using a Web 2.0 service as one would be in publishing on any other medium.

Answer to exercise 1

It depends very much on whether the contributor to the Web 2.0 service had signed the sort of contract noted immediately above. If they had done, and had they warranted that what they had put up would not cause anyone any damage, then the person who was hospitalized might have a claim against the individual for having broken their warranty, especially in view of the fact that the contract should have made them take notice of their obligations. If, on the other hand, the person who had put the misleading information in had not been forced to read and agree to such terms and conditions, the person hospitalized would have a tougher time proving their case against the individual who posted the material, and might have a better chance of suing the person running the Web 2.0 service. Either way, there is a plausible argument that the mere fact that it is well known that mushrooms can be poisonous, and that the Web 2.0 service was not the same as a publication from a reputable publisher, should have made the individual who was hospitalized cautious about accepting the advice of the Web 2.0 service and so, at minimum, have themselves partially to blame for the accident.

CHAPTER 9

Useful sources

The list of resources below is not intended to be a master list of all relevant sources of information on the topics covered in this book. Such a comprehensive list would be incomplete the day after it was written. Rather it represents those sources that I find the most useful when researching legal issues, or when responding to queries. The list includes textbooks, web-based resources and a few blogs and electronic discussion lists. I have annotated them with comments about the resource in question.

Textbooks and reference works
(These are all primarily or solely focused on UK law)

Andrews, N. (2011) *Contract Law*, Cambridge University Press.
  Standard textbook.
Armstrong, C. and Bebbington, L. (eds) (2004) *Staying Legal*, Facet Publishing.
  Despite its age, a useful set of chapters introducing concepts in information law. Aimed at library and information professionals.
Bently, L. and Sherman, B. (2009) *Intellectual Property Law*, Oxford University Press.
  Well written and comprehensive standard text.
Carey, P. (2009) *Data Protection*, Oxford University Press.
  Lots of practical guidance to the law.
Carey, P. and Turle, M. (eds) (2008) *Freedom of Information Handbook*, The Law Society.
  Series of practice-focused contributed chapters.
Cornish, W. and Llewelyn, D. (2007) *Intellectual Property*, Sweet & Maxwell.
  Standard textbook.
Derclaye, E. (2008) *The Legal Protection of Databases*, Edward Elgar.
  Useful analysis of the laws in the major countries of the world, and their rationale.
Edwards, L. (ed.) (2005) *The New Legal Framework for E-commerce in Europe*, Hart Publishing.

Although somewhat dated, useful for anyone involved in e-commerce activities within the EU.

Garnett, K. et al. (2011) *Copinger and Skone James on Copyright*, two volumes, Sweet & Maxwell.
A major reference work on copyright and related rights, widely used by lawyers. Expensive and authoritative. It has a major competitor in Vitoria et al.'s book (see below).

Jay, R. (2012) *Data Protection Law and Practice*, Sweet & Maxwell.
Comprehensive, authoritative and readable – a rare combination.

Jones, H. and Benson, C. (2006) *Publishing Law*, Routledge.
Although primarily aimed at print publishers, the law as described applies equally to any kind of electronic publishing. Readable and helpful text.

Kohl, U. (2007) *Jurisdiction and the Internet*, Cambridge University Press.
An excellent analysis of the problems – and possible solutions – raised by differences in the law in different countries.

MacQueen, H. et al. (2009) *Contemporary Intellectual Property*, Oxford University Press.
Another standard textbook.

Marchini, R. (2010) *Cloud Computing*, British Standards Institution.
Comprehensive overview of all legal issues associated with cloud computing.

Mathieson, K. (ed.) (2010) *Privacy Law Handbook*, Law Society.
Practical handbook with much useful advice.

Michaels, A. and Norris, A. (2010) *A Practical Approach to Trade Mark Law*, Oxford University Press.
Standard textbook.

Owen, L. (2010) *Clark's Publishing Agreement: a book of precedents*, Bloomsbury Professional.

Padfield, T. (2010) *Copyright for Archivists and Records Managers*, Facet Publishing.
A somewhat misleading title, as it offers an authoritative summary of the law suitable for most library and information professionals.

Poole, J. (2010) *Textbook on Contract Law*, Oxford University Press.
Title says it all!

Reed, C. and Angel, J. (eds) (2007) *Computer Law*, Oxford University Press.
Standard text.

Richards, P. (2011) *Law of Contract*, Pearson.

Room, S. (2007) *Data Protection and Compliance in Context*, British Computer Society.
Practical handbook.

Room, S. (2008) *Email Law, Practice and Compliance*, Law Society.
All aspects of UK law that apply to e-mails.

Rowland, D. et al. (2011) *Information Technology Law*, Routledge.
Comprehensive and up to date.

Sparrow, A. (2010) *The Law of Virtual Worlds and Internet Social Networks*,
Gower.
Much more on virtual worlds than social networks. Interesting discussion on
the unique legal issues raised in virtual worlds.

Stead, A. (2009) *Information Rights in Practice*, Facet Publishing.
Primarily aimed at those who own or handle information. Covers data
protection and freedom of information. Useful boxed case studies.

Stokes, S. (2009) *Digital Copyright Law and Practice*, Hart Publishing.
Readable overview.

Todd, E. (2008) *The Laws of the Internet*, Tottel Publishing.
Wide-ranging overview of legal issues.

Vitoria, M. et al. (2011) *The Modern Law of Copyright and Designs*, Lexis-Nexis.

Williams, A. et al. (2011) *Digital Media Contracts*, Oxford University Press.
A set of model contracts with commentary on them.

Web-based resources

www.web2rights.org
The best single web-based resource for all aspects of Web 2.0. It provides
legal background, risk assessment advice, toolkits, draft policy documents
and so on. The material is available under Creative Commons licences, so
can be repurposed and reused at will, as long as attribution is given.

www.jisclegal.ac.uk/Themes/CloudComputing.aspx
The entire JISC legal website is exceptionally useful for information and
commentary on legal issues relating to IT applications in higher and further
education. If you are not in those sectors, don't let that put you off – the
vast bulk of the commentary and advice applies to anyone, whatever sector
they work in. The particular part noted above relates to cloud computing.

www.jisclegal.ac.uk/ManageContent/ManageContent/tabid/243/ID/2135/
JISC-Legal-Cloud-Computing-and-the-Law-Toolkit-31082011.aspx
A typical example of the type of toolkit the JISC legal service offers.

www.jorum.ac.uk/policies/jorum-notice-and-takedown-policy
This provides a model of a 'notice and takedown' policy, which could be
used, with appropriate amendments, by any organization that maintains a
website or Web 2.0 service.

www.ico.gov.uk/for_organisations/privacy_and_electronic_communications/co
okie_rules_prepare.aspx
ICO guidance explaining what steps are needed to ensure compliance with
the new cookie regulations.

www.bigwobber.nl/wp-content/uploads/2011/10/Fringe-Special-Overview-

FOIA-oct-2011.pdf

A useful list of the state of play on FoI legislation throughout the world.

www.cloudlegal.ccls.qmul.ac.uk/Research/index.html

An excellent series of research reports on legal issues of the cloud published by Queen Mary University.

www.out-law.com/page-5700

Excellent advice for those involved in domain name disputes, although a little dated.

Blogs, Twitter feeds and discussion lists

Follow http://ipkitten.blogspot.com/ for an informed and often amusing take on all development in intellectual property law, including, inevitably, much to do with the internet and Web 2.0.

Follow @copyrightgirl (Emily Goodhand) on Twitter for remarkable coverage of international news and commentary on all aspects of copyright law, but with an emphasis on internet-related news. How she manages to collate and then re-disseminate so much news and commentary when holding down a full-time job is a mystery to me.

A number of JISCmail discussion lists are of value, especially freedom-of-information, data-protection and lis-copyseek. Contributors provide news updates, commentary on the news, and links to external resources, and frequently respond to queries posed by list members. However, not all these lists are available to anyone who wants to join; in some cases one must apply for membership, and you can be rejected if your job role does not fulfil the criteria for membership. Check www.jiscmail.ac.uk for details.

I also tweet from time to time on information law matters. You can follow me at @CharlesOppenh.

Index